THE
MIND KITCHEN

Rediscover the Power of Your Subconscious

"First Anniversary Edition."

"AN OPERATING MANUAL THAT EXPLAINS
THE SCIENCE OF HOW TO RESET YOUR MIND."

CAPT. PRATAP MEHTA

Made with ♥ on the Notion Press Platform

www.notionpress.com

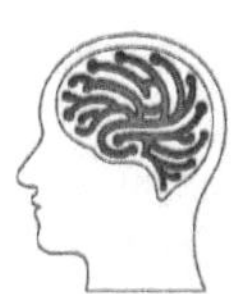

The Generous Welcome

This isn't a legal disclaimer - think of it as a friendly nudge from someone who once thought 'copyright' meant writing with your right hand.

When I began my journey as a writer, I was lit up by words left behind by generous souls - writers who gave freely, never knowing they'd be the spark in someone else's story. That's how I wish these pages to live: open, accessible, and yours to use.

Everything you find in these pages - from philosophy and story to practical technique, is offered openly. Remix, borrow, and share, no secret handshakes required. If this book were a loaf of bread, I'd want you to break off a piece and pass it along (gluten-free sharing is always encouraged).

So, take what you need, leave what you don't - like a buffet, but with fewer calories and more opportunity for growth.

All content by Capt Pratap Mehta is not protected by copyright. Attribution is appreciated, but kindness and curiosity are the only requirements.

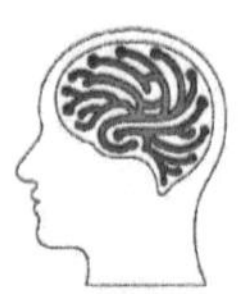

"*Transformation begins not with changing the world, but by changing the story you tell yourself each day.*"

"*If you can't change a situation, change your perception of it. Remember, most of your stress comes from the way you respond, not the way life is.*"

~ Mindretreat

Dedication

*This book is also dedicated to the
modern sages - Swami Vivekananda, Swami Parthasarathy,
Acharya S.N. Goenka, Swami Sarvapriyananda,
BK Sister Shivani, Prabhu Gaur Gopal Das,
and Janki Santoke - who have made the mysteries of the mind
a little less mysterious for the rest of us.*

*To my grandchildren, Ayrra, Sufi and Rumi,
and to all the young dreamers of planet Earth.
The future is in your hands.
May they create, explore, and lead.*

Contents

Tributes to the Author

For over a decade, Capt Pratap Mehta's MindRetreat has been more than just a program - it's been an experience of transformation. Drawing on ancient wisdom, mindful meditation, and practical affirmations, his workshops and online sessions have touched lives across continents.

These tributes come from people of diverse walks of life - professionals, students, and leaders, who have applied his teachings in their daily challenges. They speak of real results: clarity in high-pressure moments, resilience through change, and an empowered mindset that sees possibility where there was once only obstacle.

****

"Practising gratitude helps me shift my focus from problems to possibilities. Instead of dwelling on what's lacking, I start to see the strengths, support, and opportunities that already exist in my life. This perspective is the foundation of my personal growth - it builds resilience, strengthens relationships, and helps me overcome challenges with a positive, empowered mindset."

Sheetal Jogia,
Pharmacy Technician & Senior Trainer, London

"Not just about motivation, they are about practical transformation. The gratitude exercises introduced in the group have made me more mindful and appreciative in daily life, leading to noticeable improvements in my outlook and relationships."

Simranjit Kaur,
Law Student, Kuala Lumpur

"My participation in MindRetreat has transformed problem-solving from a solitary, sometimes overwhelming task into a collaborative, positive, and growth-oriented process. I now approach challenges with curiosity, creativity, and confidence, knowing I have both the mindset and the support network to find effective solutions."

Pravesh Sawon,
Senior Manager, L&D Institute, Mauritius

"The daily gratitude practices, sharing of small wins, and encouragement from peers made participants feel accountable and inspired to take consistent action. This sense of community and mutual support helped me push through periods of low motivation or self-doubt."

Unnati Priya,
National Bronze Medallist – 2024 (Manipuri Martial Art), Jharkhand

"MindRetreat has helped me bring mindfulness into my busy urban life. The practical techniques and supportive community have made it possible for me to manage stress, stay positive, and find balance, even amidst the daily demands of work and family."

Usha Sukumaran,
Educator & Grandmother, Melbourne, Australia

"I've discovered that gratitude is a powerful force for personal growth. When I make it a habit to genuinely appreciate the people around me, I notice a shift in my own mindset and energy.

Prerana Sharma,
Physiotherapy Student, Udaipur

These are just a few voices from the MindRetreat community, where real people experience real transformation – one mindful step at a time.

Introduction

~ Rediscover Your Mind's Hidden Power ~

Welcome to *The Mind Kitchen: Rediscover the Power of Your Subconscious.* If this book is in your hands, you're likely searching for life's operating manual, the practical guide to unlock your true potential. I'm delighted you've found your way here.

The Afternoon Everything Changed

Picture this: Jodhpur Air Force Flying Academy, late afternoon, nine months into rigorous flying training. Suspension hits like a thunderbolt. Around me, joyful Flight Cadets celebrate solo flights over beer mugs. I'm alone in my darkness, the buzz of rejection fading into heavy silence.

That moment crystallised everything. Enough was enough. I turned down the navigation branch offer and went home. Three days later, a telegram from Naval Headquarters. Join the Indian Navy. The rest, as they say, is history. That pivot taught me: **the mind can turn rejection into redirection when you decide to change.**

Baptised in Mindfulness

My fascination with the mind began at 15 in Jaipur. My uncle arranged a Swami from Bihar School of Yoga to live with us for a month. We shared a bedroom - I meditated, ate, slept yoga. Endless discussions on pranayama, Dhyan, Vedanta. I was immersed.

Years later, Swami Vivekananda's commentaries on Patanjali's Yoga Sutras lit the fire. Masters like Maharishi Patanjali, Acharya Mahapragya, Swami Parthasarathy, and Acharya SN Goenka shaped my path. After 30 years in the Navy, this passion became my mission: **MindRetreat-equipping leaders with inner tools for outer success.**

The Power of Faith

(Adapted from traditional wisdom)

> *"Raise your thoughts like a guiding light,*
>
> *Dreams take wing when vision is bright.*
>
> *Trust your journey, trust your heart's plan,*
>
> *For change begins with the mind of man.*
>
> *Strength is not in wealth or might,*
>
> *But in hope that turns dark to light.*
>
> *The prize goes not to swifter feet,*
>
> *But to those who never accept defeat."*

This power shines brightest in Prime Minister Narendra Modi's life. From humble chaiwallah to uniting 1.4 billion Indians through conviction alone. **Belief, not circumstance, forges destiny.** This spirit fills every chapter. Awakening your highest potential, wherever you begin.

What will you learn here?

In this revolutionary book, 'THE MIND KITCHEN – Rediscover the Power of Your Subconscious, you will learn all these techniques and more. All your hard work towards success can get drowned in the ocean of noise if you don't have the right mindset strategies.

This book is a compilation of incidents and experiences that have taught me invaluable lessons. This book also compiles many course contents and the scripts delivered in workshops and talks during the past twenty years. Hence, you may find the writing style to be like spoken English. Each chapter is my take on widely discussed topics.

Your Practical Mind Manual

Thousands of books launch yearly. Why this one? *The Mind Kitchen* distils 20 years training executives, educators, students, homemakers. Workshop scripts become spoken-style chapters blending Vedic wisdom, neuroscience, positive psychology.

As Naval Ravikant notes: *"To write a great book, you must first become the book."* (Twitter/X, May 15, 2018).

No theory fluff. Expect: Concrete techniques (breathwork, visualisation, anchoring). Real stories (mine and others'). Daily habits for lasting change.

Think of this as your **mental kitchen**. Stock it with empowering ingredients, cook consistently, feast on transformation. No robes or PhDs needed. Just curiosity and commitment.

Like my Navy pivot or Modi's rise, **small mental shifts create seismic life changes.** Ready to restock your kitchen?

Captain Pratap Mehta

Founder, MindRetreat Academy

Mumbai

How to Use This Book

Welcome to your MindRetreat journey - a practical guide to weaving mindful meditation, affirmations and ancient wisdom into the fabric of your daily life. This book is designed not just for reading, but for doing, reflecting, and transforming.

- **Read Actively, Reflect Deeply**: Each chapter blends mythological stories, practical insights, and step-by-step exercises. Pause after each story or lesson to reflect on how it relates to your own life.

- **Practice as You Learn**: You'll find mindful meditation and affirmation exercises throughout the book. Don't rush - give yourself permission to pause, close your eyes, and actually try the techniques as you encounter them. Even a few minutes of practice can make a difference.

- **Personalise Your Routine**: There is no one-size-fits-all approach. Use the sample routines and personalisation tips to create a daily or weekly practice that fits your unique rhythms and needs. Try pairing exercises with existing habits - such as mindful breathing while making tea or a gratitude reflection before bed.

- **Engage with the Tools**: The appendices offer a toolkit of mind programming tips, further reading, and practical resources. Use these sections as a reference whenever you want to deepen your practice or explore new techniques.

- **Share Your Journey**: Consider discussing your experiences with a friend, family member, or fellow seeker. Sharing insights and challenges not only deepens your understanding but also builds a supportive community around your personal growth.

Remember: This book is your companion on the path from inspiration to transformation. Use it at your own pace, return to it often, and let each exercise, story, and affirmation guide you towards a more mindful, resilient, and joyful life.

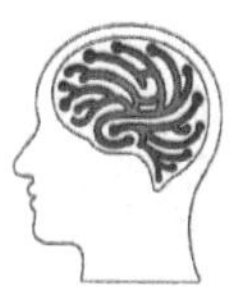

1

Mind and Indian Philosophy

~ From Atom to Cosmos: Indian Wisdom for Mastering the Mind.

Foundations For Mind Mastery

Each of us has been bestowed with a unique purpose and a wellspring of compassion, along with a mind teeming with ideas. My reflections in this chapter arise from two profound sources: the ancient wisdom of Indian philosophy and the contemporary insights of positive psychology and neuroscience. Together, they invite us to explore the nature and power of the mind.

At the heart of Indian philosophical thought lies a practical model for resetting the mind built on three pillars: self-awareness, objectivity, and equanimity. These principles form the foundational laws of behavioural transformation. Readers familiar with Vedic or Buddhist traditions will recognise their resonance in concepts like Mindfulness, Vipassana, and Preksha Dhyan - practices that harness the immense abilities of our subconscious.

The Upanishads and the Mind's Infinite Potential

Ancient scriptures like the Upanishads offer timeless wisdom about the mind's extraordinary capabilities. To understand this, we turn to the epic Mahabharata, a saga central to Indian cultural heritage. Within it pulses the Bhagavad Gita, a dialogue between Prince Arjuna and his divine guide Krishna amid an epic family conflict. This profound scripture grapples with duty, choice, and the power of inner transformation.

A thought-provoking question arises: why were these life-changing teachings granted to Arjuna, and not his adversary, Duryodhana? Could history have been altered if the antagonist had embraced such wisdom?

Krishna & Duryodhana

In the Mahabharata, Krishna did in fact caution Duryodhana, reminding him that his path was *Adharma* (unrighteousness). Duryodhana's reply is striking. He admitted, with brutal honesty:

"I know what is right, yet I do not act on it. I know what is wrong, yet I cannot resist doing it. Desire and impulse drag me onward. I cannot control myself. That is my struggle."

This is not just Duryodhana's plight but humanity's condition. We all have faced this inner conflict.

Now compare this with Arjuna's response in the Gita. Arjuna too confesses:

"What you ask me to do is difficult. My impulses, my passions, my anger – they pull me astray. How can I walk the path of Dharma?"

The difference is subtle yet profound:

Duryodhana: *"This is who I am. I cannot change."*

Arjuna: *"This is who I am. How can I change? Teach me."*

It is this openness, this willingness to transform that makes Arjuna the hero and the worthy recipient of Krishna's wisdom.

Reflections

This distinction between resisting change and seeking change, is what decides our growth. Teachers, philosophers, psychologists, and counsellors can all serve as guides, but their wisdom benefits us only when we decide to help ourselves.

The very first step in your personal transformation is this choice: To recognise your condition, and then ask, *"How can I be better?"*

Do You Have a Plan for Self-Development?

Ralph J. Cordiner, chairman of General Electric, once told a leadership conference: *"We need from every man who aspires to leadership, for himself and his company – a determination to undertake a personal program of self-development. Nobody can order a man to develop. Whether a man lags or advances in his speciality depends on his own application. It requires time, work, and sacrifice. Nobody can do it for you."*

Cordiner's words are timeless and practical. Live them. People in every field – business, engineering, the arts, writing, spirituality, or public service, rise to the top by committing to self-development.

Any training program must do three things:

Provide meaningful content – *what to do.*

Supply a clear method – *how to do it.*

Pass the acid test – achieving *results.*

The What in your personal training program is built on the attitudes and techniques of successful people. How do they manage themselves? How do they overcome obstacles? What earns them respect and influence? What thoughts distinguish them from the ordinary?

The How of personal growth is presented throughout this book – concrete action steps in each chapter. Apply them, test them, and witness the difference yourself.

And the Results? With careful and consistent application, you can achieve success on scales that may now seem impossible. Broken into its components, your program for success will yield:

- Deeper respect from your family

- Admiration from friends and associates

- Fulfilment from being useful and making a difference

- Material rewards: higher income and a better standard of living

Concept of Mind

Who First Introduced the Idea of the Mind? The origin of the mind has fascinated philosophers for thousands of years. Who first introduced this concept? Let us begin by drawing a parallel with another question:

Who discovered the Atom? Many would say John Dalton, who reintroduced the atomic theory in 1800. Before him, the Greek philosopher Democritus had considered the idea of atoms around 450 BC.

In India, Maharishi Patanjali described the concept of the atom in his *Yoga Sutras* - over two thousand years ago. Patanjali, who lived during the second century BC, authored this seminal text on Yoga theory and practice.

Patanjali's Yoga Sutra

In the *Yoga Sutras*, Patanjali explains that mastery over the mind encompasses everything, from the atom to the cosmos. Sutra 40 (Vibhuti Pada):

परमाणु परममहत्तान्तोऽस्य वशीकारः।

Transliteration: *paramāṇu parama mahattvānto 'sya vaśhī kāraḥ*

Mastering the mind results in control of the relationship with everything from the atom to the cosmos.

चित्त के शांत होने पर अणु से लेकर सम्पूर्ण ब्रह्माण्ड तक की समझ उत्पन्न होती है।

Swami Vivekananda's Commentary:

"The Yogi's mind, thus meditating, becomes unobstructed, from the atomic to the Infinite. Through such practice, the mind can easily contemplate both the minute and the vast, and its restless waves gradually subside."

Thus, Patanjali introduces the ageless truth: a focused mind is limitless in its capacity to perceive, create, and transform.

The Body as a Flux of Atoms

Our physical body is not as solid or fixed as it appears. It is a constantly changing flow of atoms, activated by consciousness - just as the sun energises the entire planet. The characteristics of our body are:

- Our skin replaces itself every 28 days.

- The lining of our gut regenerates every 72 hours.

- Each cell contains 100 billion atoms, each buzzing with subatomic movement.

So, when you look at your body, remember it is never the same from one moment to the next.

In the same way, every object in the external world is also in continuous atomic flux. So how can the moving atoms of our body relate to the shifting atoms of outside objects?

The Role of Meditation: Becoming the Pure Observer

Through the practice of meditation, we intentionally step back from our habitual identification with the ever-changing body and the continuously moving universe. By doing so, we enter a state of pure observation, where we are no longer entangled with the fluctuations of our physical form or the external environment. In this state, we remain as the witness, calmly observing without attachment or reaction.

This witnessing awareness is what Patanjali refers to as Samvedna (sensations) - a state of uninterrupted, continuous sensation. In Samvedna, the mind experiences reality directly, unobstructed by mental restlessness or distraction. By cultivating this pure observer state through meditation, we begin to experience the true nature of existence. It is a seamless flow of sensation and awareness, beyond the limitations of the body and the fleeting world around us.

Mind and Brain: The Science Behind It

In modern science, the brain and mind are often compared to computer hardware and software:

The **brain** is like the hardware - the CPU that processes inputs and executes tasks.

The **mind** is the software - it programs logic, decision-making, and perception.

But Indian philosophy adds depth to this analogy: the body is the supercomputer, the brain a storage and processing unit, and the mind the subtle software that links the physical and the conscious. Without the mind's "programming," the brain alone cannot function meaningfully; likewise, the body without consciousness is only inert machinery.

Neuroscientist Caroline Leaf captures this well: "The mind and brain are different but intertwined. The mind is energy that creates energy through thinking, feeling, and choosing." This explains why:

People with strong neural connections (robust wiring) learn faster, perform better, and build lasting relationships.

Those with weaker connections may struggle, often leading to negative cycles such as addiction or frustration.

Indian philosophy often distinguishes between the physical body (sharira), the mind–intellect complex (manas), and the deeper consciousness or self (atman). The brain is seen as part of the material body, while the mind is subtler and linked to consciousness. This metaphor helps bridge ancient wisdom with contemporary understandings of mind and body.

The hopeful truth is profound: the mind can reshape and rewire the brain, transforming personality and behaviour through intentional practice. This interplay between mind, brain, and body is the cornerstone of true personal transformation.

The Brain is Not Fixed

Until the late 20th century, scientists believed the brain stopped developing around age sixteen, after which it was "hardwired." Change was thought to be impossible.

But neuroscience now confirms the remarkable concept of neuroplasticity: *Dormant connections in the brain can be reactivated, and meditation is a proven, natural way to do so.*

Indian sages knew this long ago:

- Maharishi Valmiki was once a feared dacoit. By practising meditation (Dhyan), he transformed into a seer and composed the *Ramayana.*

- Kalidas, once mocked as a fool, rose to become one of India's greatest poets through years of sadhana (spiritual practice).

Such transformations remind us that meditation is not limited to saints, it is possible for anyone willing to reprogram the mind.

Consciousness and Brain Activity

What is consciousness? At its simplest: awareness. Awareness of yourself (inner) and the world (outer).

Success in life requires tapping into all sides of the brain:

- The creative, intuitive right brain

- The logical, analytical left brain

Brain activity corresponds with shifts in consciousness. The four main brainwave patterns are:

Outer Focus (Conscious Mind) – relating to the external world

Beta: fast, alert, logical thinking (13+ cycles/sec)

Inner Focus (Subconscious Mind) – thoughts, imagination, intuition

Alpha: relaxed alertness, learning, intuition (8–12 c/s)

Theta: deep meditation and creativity (5–7 c/s)

Unconscious Mind – automatic body functions (heartbeat, digestion)

Delta: slowest waves, deep sleep (<4 c/s)

How Does Mindful Meditation Work?

Like a computer, the mind can be programmed but it requires daily maintenance. Just as food and exercise nourish the body, meditation nourishes and protects the mind, acting as its "anti-virus" against negativity.

By meditating, we:

- Observe thoughts, even negative ones like anxiety, anger, or depression.

- Neutralise their power, simply through awareness.

- Choose consciously which thoughts to keep, which to let go, and which to transform.

Over time, this strengthens self-control, attention, and emotional regulation, replacing harmful mental habits with empowering ones.

The result?

- Healthier relationships with ourselves and others

- Greater empathy and compassion

- Stronger memory and learning abilities

- Freedom from limiting beliefs and behaviours

Meditation is thus not an escape, but a deeply practical tool for rewiring the brain and reshaping our lives. Mindful meditation trains us to pause and observe the mind instead of running on autopilot. As our understanding grows, an important question arises: what are the channels through which we experience the world? To answer that, we turn to the five senses and why they matter so much.

What are my five senses?

Let me share a story.

One day, a person climbed a mountain where a hermit was meditating. This person sought shelter in the hermitage and asked the saint for help.

"What are you doing here alone in such a lonely place?" To which the saint replied, "I have lots of work."

Surprised, the person asked, "How can you have so much work? I don't see anything here."

The saint smiled and said, "I have to train two hawks and two eagles, assure two rabbits, discipline one snake, motivate a donkey and tame a lion..."

Person: "Where have they gone? I don't see them." Saint: "I have them all here within my body!"

The hawks stare at everything presented to me, good or bad; I must work on them to see only good things. They are my eyes.

The two eagles' claws hurt and destroy, so I must train them not to break. They are my hands.

The Rabbits want to go where they want but do not want to face tricky situations. I must teach them to be calm even if they suffer or stumble. They are my feet.

The donkey is always tired and stubborn and does not want to carry the load whenever I walk. That is my body.

The most difficult to tame is the "snake." Although it is locked in a strong cage with thirty-two bars, it is always ready to sting, bite and poison anyone nearby. I must discipline it... that's my tongue.

I also have one Lion. Oh ... immensely proud, full of vanity. He thinks that "he is the king." I must tame him. And that's my ego.

So, you see, my friend, I have lots of work. And you, what do you work on? Think about it...! Mindful living begins with understanding the "inner animals" we manage every day - our senses, body, tongue, and ego. The real question then becomes: how do we retrain this entire inner zoo? That's where the backbone of mind reset comes in - the three-step discipline of self-awareness, objectivity, and equanimity, grounded in the timeless insights of Indian philosophy.

What is the backbone of mind reset?

The backbone of Indian philosophy is the three-step model of mind reset: self-awareness, objectivity, and equanimity - the three laws of behavioural change that evolve out of these steps. Readers with Vedic and Buddhist backgrounds may recognise some of these terms as the power of the sub-conscience mind, which has been popularised more recently as Mindfulness (West), Vipassana (Buddhism), and Preksha Dhyan (Jainism).

Indian philosophy can be introduced in various ways but always begins with "The Vedas". Hinduism, known as Sanatan Dharma, is the world's oldest religion and part of Indian philosophy. Many of the current adaptations of Hinduism used in 'Western Spirituality' today, such as Karma, chakras, third eye, manifestation, and yoga, have their roots in this ancient religion. Ancient Eastern religions are in danger of being forgotten about and denied credit for many everyday spiritual activities due to the popularity of 'Western Spirituality'.

Karma is a concept in Indian philosophy that has several definitions. The common sayings, "what goes around comes around' and 'what you sow is what you reap', with notable examples of how Karma works, will be discussed later in the book. Dharma denotes behaviours considered the right way of living, which is righteousness.

Chapter Summary

In this chapter, we explored the timeless quest to understand the *mind* – from ancient Indian philosophy to modern neuroscience.

Patanjali's Yoga Sutra teaches that mastery over the mind connects everything from the *Atom to the Cosmos*. True concentration enables us to perceive both the tiniest and the infinite.

- The body itself is not static but a flux of atoms, constantly regenerating, reminding us that change is built into nature.

- The mind and brain are different: the brain is hardware, the mind is the software that directs it. Neuroscience now supports what yogis knew for centuries – meditation can literally reshape neural wiring.

- Consciousness operates at different levels – conscious, subconscious, and unconscious. Each has corresponding brainwave states – Beta, Alpha, Theta, and Delta.

- Meditation is the practical bridge. By observing, choosing, and redirecting our thoughts, we reprogram the mind, heal emotions, and transform behaviour.

- Neuroplasticity: Thoughts and meditation create new brain pathways even after 16 – change is always possible.

Reflect & Apply

Try these steps: Use these prompts to integrate the chapter into daily life:

Awareness check:

Notice one recurring thought today. Is it positive, neutral, or negative?

Do not fight it; simply observe it with curiosity.

Reframe the thought:

If the thought is negative (for example, "I can't do this"), soften it into a supportive reframe like, "I am learning to handle this step by step."

Meditation micro-practice:

Sit still for 2 minutes and rest your attention on the natural flow of your breath.

When a thought appears, silently label it "thinking" and gently return to the breath.

Journaling prompt:

Note one limiting belief you hold and one empowering belief you would like to adopt instead.

Reflect: *How would my life change if I consistently lived from this empowering belief?*

Mastery of life begins with mastery of the mind. Your inner kitchen is stocked with thoughts, emotions, and attention and whatever you keep "cooking" there is what you end up living.

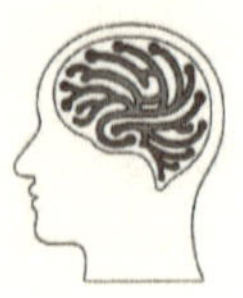

2

Understanding Mind

~ A mind in its place and in itself can make a heaven of hell
and hell of heaven.

The Eternal Battle Within

Modern sages and contemporary teachers like Swami Vivekananda, Swami Parthasarathy, Acharya S. N. Goenka and Swami Sarvapriyananda, all echo one timeless insight: our thoughts, attitudes, and beliefs quietly script the way we live, love, and lead. These inner patterns determine whether the same situation becomes a battlefield of stress or a training ground for wisdom.

Why is it that some people radiate peace and joy in the middle of hardship, while others feel empty and restless even when life appears comfortable from the outside? To understand this, the Mahabharata offers a powerful metaphor. The great war on Kurukshetra is not just a historical conflict; it symbolises the inner war between our higher qualities - courage, compassion, clarity and our lower impulses - anger, fear, attachment, and doubt.

Arjuna, the mighty warrior, collapses in the chariot, paralysed by confusion and moral conflict. Krishna, his divine charioteer, does not fight the battle for him; instead, he awakens Arjuna to a profound truth: "The real battleground is the mind, and the real power lies in choice."

In each moment, the same mind can chain us through negativity, or free us through wisdom.

Understanding the Mind

Understanding the mind is the starting point of all inner work. Drawing on a talk by Swami Sarvapriyananda (Ramakrishna Order), resident minister at the Vedanta Society of New York, and on Bhagavad Gita and Vedanta classes with my teacher Janki Santoke, a senior disciple of Swami Parthasarathy, this section explores that inner terrain.

At its core, the mind is a powerful instrument for decision-making, concentration, and selfless action. The first key theme is the **transformative power of conscious choice** - the capacity to direct one's life by choosing thoughts, responses, and values with awareness. This power is innate in all of us, yet it often remains dormant or underused until we learn how to engage it deliberately.

Power of Decision

We all have the power to decide but rarely use it fully. In Bhagavad Gita, Krishna calls the enemy within us *our own passions, anger, and rage* - present in saint and sinner alike. The difference?

"Do not give way to them," Krishna tells Arjuna, that's the path to despair and destruction.

A saint feels anger but consciously chooses not to act on it.

Most people function on autopilot - a lifetime of conditioned behaviours, ingrained like software in a computer's boot sequence. When trouble arrives, the default reactions of irritation or rage play out unconsciously, like an old program running itself.

Swami Sarvapriyananda teaches us there exists a *brief window* - a tiny moment when these unconscious reactions surface into conscious awareness but before they manifest externally. Within this fleeting opportunity, you can choose to reject automatic responses and replace them with wiser thoughts and actions.

For instance, when the urge to check your phone arises, you may habitually obey. Or you might pause, say no, and focus on the present moment instead. That pause is conscious choice - your power in action.

Exercising Our Decision Power

Consciously saying no to one thing and yes to another throughout your day is the transformative practice. Yet, most of us hardly practice this consciously for ourselves.

Think: When tempted to interrupt a meeting with a phone check, can you say no and stay present? Offered a second helping of dessert, can you say no and honour your health?

Krishna calls this waking into *conscious action* - not just random choices, but decisions with awareness and intention.

Vivekananda said: *"Power will come when the sleeping soul is roused to conscious action. Glory and goodness arrive when the soul awakens to deliberate choice."*

So why not consciously say yes to what you want in life - clear about what enriches you and no to what doesn't serve you?

Mindful Choices Shape Life

Krishna points to four levels of choice:

- What thoughts we entertain

- What words we use

- What we speak

- What actions we take

Thoughts are the subtlest, actions the most visible outcome. Guard your thoughts and words, and your actions will follow naturally.

A Pebble Exercise for Mind Training

A student monk once confessed meditation was difficult because of unwanted thoughts. His teacher gave him a simple exercise:

- Take a black pebble and drop one in a bowl each time an unwanted thought appears.

- Take a white pebble and drop one for each pure or spiritual thought.

At first, the bowl filled with black pebbles. But with persistent practice, white pebbles began to dominate.

The message is clear: *By consciously observing and choosing our thoughts, we can reshape our entire mental and behavioural landscape.*

This section reminds us that the magic lies less in controlling what thoughts arise and more in consciously deciding which to nurture or dismiss - the power of choice is always ours.

Power of Concentration

Let's delve into the immense power of concentration or focused attention. Swami Vivekananda once said that the difference between an ordinary person and a great person often boils down to the depth of their concentration. At first, I was sceptical - could it really be *just* about focus? But then, a story shifted my perspective entirely.

Swami Sarvapriyananda recounts an incident involving a young monk preparing for one of India's toughest exams, the IIT entrance - ranked second among thousands. One day, a senior monk approached and saw the young monk reading with ease, lounging comfortably with his foot resting on the bed. Twice the senior asked, "What are you reading?" but the young monk said nothing. Finally, the senior monk grabbed the young monk's big toe, yet the younger monk didn't flinch, completely absorbed in his reading. That moment of total immersion - that undistracted focus, was the essence of concentration.

We all know such individuals in our midst - whether in academics, arts, science, or meditation. They rare few who can lock their attention unwaveringly on the task at hand.

A Hungaria American psychologist Mihaly Csikszentmihalyi, author of the classic *Flow*, devoted his life to understanding concentration. He explains that the human mind can consciously process roughly 120 bits of information per second. This modest bandwidth includes body awareness, breathing, environment, and mental state. Concentration means directing as much of these 120 bits as possible to a single object - be it a book, music, or work.

Nowadays, children often struggle with focus. Parents complain about kids studying with rock music blasting, texting, or browsing the web simultaneously and becoming upset if those distractions are taken away. Today's kids grow up in constant engagement, but this rarely translates into deep concentration. They're trained to be distracted rather than focused.

Daniel Goleman, the emotional intelligence expert, champions meditation as a powerful tool to train children and adults in concentration. It's encouraging that meditation is gaining respect in modern psychology as a path to sharpen focus and clarity.

Ancient Wisdom Meets Modern Science

Mihaly also notes that classical literature worldwide, East and West, cherishes *flow experiences* - states of deep, energised concentration. He specifically praises Patanjali's *Yoga Sutra* as the best-known system for generating flow.

The *Yoga Sutra* is more than a study technique; it's a blueprint for enlightenment. Its second sutra guides us toward *dhyana* - uninterrupted stream of thoughts leading to deep contemplation.

Patanjali's method is a remarkable technology for focus:

- First come the moral disciplines, *Yama* and *Niyama*.

- Then, learning to sit quietly, like holding a bowl of water without stirring it.

- When the body is still, the mind can be still; focus follows.

Swami Sarvapriyananda recalls a Himalayan monk's strict meditation drill: *"He barked out commands in Hindi like a drill sergeant: 'Don't move, don't speak, don't think!' Three stages to silence - the body first, then the mental chatter, then the deeper layers of mind."*

Breath links body and mind - notice how anger brings rapid breathing, calm brings slow, even breaths. Controlling breath calms mind, and calming mind harmonises breath.

Where You Place Your Attention: Shapes Your Life

Deepak Chopra writes: *"The quality of your life depends on what you pay attention to. Are you focusing on your work, creativity, relationships, or God - or on sorrow, pain, and aging?"*

Dwelling on negatives dims life; turning the face to the sun brightens it.

John Milton captured it well: *"A mind in its place and in itself can make a heaven of hell and hell of heaven."*

The power lies in *shifting* your attention. What do you choose to dwell upon? How much do you feed your heaven or your hell?

This section highlights that concentration is not mystical but a trainable skill rooted in ancient wisdom and verified by modern science. It shapes everything from academic success to the quality of our daily experience.

Power of Selflessness

Let's talk about selflessness - not just working hard but working with heart.

Years ago, I served as liaison officer for Mr. N.A. Palkhiwala, then India's top jurist and a lover of libraries. Watching officers at Defence Services Staff College buried in books, I tried to impress him: "They read for up to 10 hours a day! That's concentration, the kind that powers the armed forces."

Palkhiwala calmly replied, "Commander, I'm not impressed."

I was floored. "Why not?" He explained: "Yes, they're focused and hardworking, but without heart. It does them no good, nor society."

He quickly adds, "Many will chase their careers, become Brigadiers and Generals, and try to make much money. They have no higher dimensions in life. They don't look around society. Even their workplace, who needs what help?"

He looked at my blank face and said, "Commander! read Vivekananda." These words of Palkhiwala touched my heart. Just an unending focus, immense power of concentration, yet without heart. Without love. Without sensibility. Without sensitivity. That's what you are describing as a demon. You are not telling a soldier.

So, along with the power of concentration is the power of *selflessness*. Swami Vivekanand, who spoke about selflessness, gave this slogan: "Work for your enlightenment and the welfare of the world." I often discuss this with my colleagues: Why the word 'and'? Why not for your enlightenment or just for the welfare of the world? Why both terms at the same time?

In the Bible, people asked Jesus, "Which is the most important of the commandments? In Judaism, they have more than 500 commandments. Which is the most important?"

Jesus says, "The most important commandment is, "Thou shalt love the Lord, thy God, with all thy heart and mind." Just as you would think the disciples were closing their notebooks, Jesus said, "**And** love thy neighbour. "Look, two things. He could have just said love thy neighbour, or he could have just said love God, but he said **both**.

Janki Santoke, a senior disciple of Swami Parthasarathy, says, "In the Gita when Krishna is summarising his teachings for Arjuna, he says contemplate in me, that is God, **and** fight the battle of life." You see a deep absorption in God and yet being involved in society and life. Not just one of the two. Not just going away. You must come back to society.

That's why you see the connection, whether Jesus says love thy God **and** love thy neighbour. Whether Krishna says, contemplate in God **and** fight the battle of life, do your duty in life. Swami Vivekananda also gives us the motto for your enlightenment **and** the world's welfare.

At the deepest level, we are not two separate entities but rather two expressions of the same reality. Swami Ramakrishna, when asked about spirituality, replied, "When I close my eyes in meditation, I find peace within. When I open my eyes, my focus shifts to asking, what can I do for you?"

That is spirituality. Both must be together. Usually, it is the other way around. Many disturbances exist when I close my eyes in the temple or church. There is no peace within. It's not what I can do for you but what I can get from you. No wonder we do not have peace. Our attitude is usually the opposite of spirituality.

One young man came to Vivekananda and said, "Swami, I tried to meditate. I closed all the doors and windows and sat and meditated for long hours. Yet I am most unhappy." Vivekananda said, "Open the doors and windows of your house. Go out and see if there is a sick person who needs help. See if there is an ignorant person who needs education. Help! Then you will get the peace you are seeking."

Janki Santoke, a senior disciple of Swami Parthasarathy, insightfully remarks, "Scriptures give us the meaning of life. That meaning is found in serving others, true concern beyond oneself. This selflessness, though often overlooked, is the highest form of maturity, and ultimately, the most rewarding path."

With this understanding, we arrive at the Real Game-Changer.

Communication With Mind

At some point, we all reach a crossroads - having tried faith, patience, and even more mysterious pursuits like black magic, yet still feeling stuck. Some people manage to find joy and contentment despite adversity, while others, comfortable and wealthy, remain perpetually dissatisfied and complaining. What separates the triumphant from the defeated?

Reflect on these emblematic lives:

- Helen Keller, who despite profound blindness and poverty, became an inspiration to millions. How did she triumph?

- Marilyn Monroe, who, despite fame and fortune, met a tragic end. What happened?

- Amitabh Bachchan, who survived a near-fatal accident during the shooting of 'Coolie,' and chose to see it as part of a larger purpose, transforming his outlook and life's trajectory.

The key difference lies not in circumstance but in how we communicate with our own minds during times of trial and the actions that flow from that internal dialogue.

To bring this truth into focus, here's a story for you…

The Seven Wonders: A Lesson in Gratitude

Mira, a bright 9-year-old from a small village near Jaisalmer in Rajasthan, was thrilled to start school in town after passing grade 4. On her first day, she faced the typical city-school dilemma, kids making fun of her simple clothes. The teacher quickly settled the class and sprang a surprise test: *"Write down the seven wonders of the world."*

All the kids rushed to write answers they'd learned - Great Wall of China, Colosseum, Taj Mahal, and more. Mira took her time, hesitating.

When asked why, she said, "There are so many wonders… how can I choose only seven?"

The teacher accepted her paper along with the others and read them aloud. Then came Mira's unique answer:

"The Seven Wonders are - to be able to See, to Hear, to Feel, to Laugh, to Think, to be Kind, to Love, and to Breathe."

Silence in the room. The teacher smiled, touched by the innocent wisdom.

Reflections on Everyday Miracles

This story reminds us: miracles surround us yet often go unnoticed. We tend to chase *more* - more possessions, more fame, more stuff, while forgetting to appreciate the *miracle* of being alive.

Two choices present themselves:

- Life is ordinary, and miracles don't exist.

- Life is miraculous, and every moment is awe-inspiring.

Choose to see miracles in the mundane. Begin with gratitude for senses and simple joys often taken for granted.

As the saying goes, you never truly value what you have until it's lost. But really, the treasure has always been within you. Your very existence is the greatest miracle.

Try adopting mindfulness, observe the small wonders daily and marvel at your own life. When you nurture this appreciation, miracles become the natural rhythm of your days.

Why Understand Your Mind?

Understanding your mind is the foundation for a joyful, balanced life. Here are ten practical steps to begin with:

- Start your day right. Avoid frantic, rushed mornings - they set the tone for the day.

- Prioritise your goals. Reset your mind daily to focus on what truly matters - be it success, relationships, or health.

- Define balance for yourself. Your sense of harmony is unique - clarify what balance means for you.

- Say yes to saying no. Don't overcommit; protect your energy and boundaries.

- Schedule time out. Regular breaks - walks, silence, and nature help refresh your mind.

- Set and maintain boundaries. Early boundary-setting transforms your professional and personal growth.

- Disconnect to reconnect. Reduce screen time; listen to your inner voice.

- Let go. Release ego, control needs, judgments, and others' expectations.

- Cut through excuses. Stop saying "I must," "I can't," or "I don't have time." These phrases drain energy and cause burnout.

- Be your own VIP. Self-care isn't selfish - make yourself a priority to truly thrive.

By embracing these steps, you nurture your mind's wellbeing and unlock the potential to live fully aware of life's deepest wonders that you already possess.

Chapter Summary

This chapter explores the power of conscious choice, showing how thoughts, attitudes, and beliefs shape behaviour and ultimately determine the quality of life. Drawing from Vedanta, the Bhagavad Gita, and modern behavioural science, it explains that the mind is not fixed; it can be trained, rewired, and refined to support growth, balance, and purpose.

Key ideas to carry forward are:

- The human mind can adapt and reorganise itself by altering the connections between brain cells; mindful meditation becomes a practical tool for steering this process and reshaping **attitudes, emotions, and behaviours.**

- People who succeed do not have fewer problems than those who struggle; the real difference lies in how they converse with their own minds and the choices they act on.

- The mind expresses three great powers: the **power of decision**, the **power of concentration**, and the **power of selflessness**.

- Captured in Swami Vivekananda's call to "Work for your own enlightenment **and** the welfare of the world."

- Ancient wisdom now converges with modern neuroscience, showing that **consciousness and focused attention** can be deliberately cultivated to achieve mental mastery rather than remaining at the mercy of conditioning.

- The chapter ultimately invites you to become more aware of your inner landscape so you can **consciously shape your mind**, and with it, your emotional stability, relationships, and direction in life.

Reflect and Apply

- **Notice your mental autopilot:** Through the day, observe moments when you react without thinking. Which impulses - anger, distraction, craving, most often derail your focus?

- **Practise the decision window:** When a strong thought or emotion arises, pause before speaking or acting and experiment with choosing a wiser response.

- **Begin simple mindfulness:** Spend 5 minutes daily observing your breath or body sensations without judgment; each time the mind wanders, gently return to your chosen point of focus.

- **Set small daily intentions:** Before key tasks, set an inner stance such as, "I will approach this with calm, clarity, and kindness," training the mind to show up deliberately.

- **Engage with wisdom texts:** Reflect on verses from the Gita or teachings on meditation that resonate with you and explore how they can illuminate present-day challenges.

By integrating these practices, you gradually build the inner discipline to direct your mind consciously and grow into your best self.

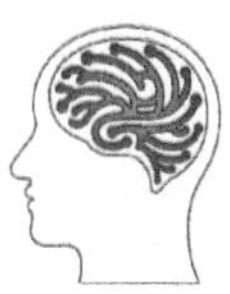

3

Power of Breath

~ Practice of breath-awareness leads to equanimity and objectivity in life.

A Journey to Mindfulness

If you've ever wondered why the world suddenly can't stop talking about "mindfulness," don't blame the latest Silicon Valley apps. This ancient wisdom traces its roots back over two and a half millennia when great sage like Lord Buddha handed down simple, practical instructions - long before hashtags and TED Talks existed.

They taught a recipe delicious in its simplicity: breathe mindfully, savour the present moment, and gradually untangle the sticky web of suffering that so often holds us captive. Over centuries, traditions like Buddhist Vipassana with its *Anapana* practice and Jain *Preksha Dhyan* emerged. Each is offering unique flavours of mindful breathing aimed at calming and liberating the restless mind. Let's imagine a little story that captures this essence.

Timeless Power of Breath

A young monk, new to meditation, felt overwhelmed by a swarm of distracting thoughts. One day, his teacher handed him a humble task. "Observe your breath," he instructed. "Follow it in...and out. When your mind wanders, gently bring it back. Your breath is always with you, a constant friend in the chaos."

The monk wasn't impressed at first, after all, breathing was automatic and ordinary. But over time, as his awareness deepened, that simple, ever-present breath became an anchor - a gateway to peace, clarity, and freedom.

This is the heart of mindfulness, not some trendy escape or a mere productivity trick but the act of "paying attention, on purpose". Forget debates about quantum consciousness or musings about what the cat thinks of you. If you can simply hold your mind gently on the rhythm of your breath at the nostrils, congratulations! You've found a remarkable anchor in the ever-shifting sea of life. And the best part? It's always free and always available, no subscription required.

What is Mindfulness?

Mindfulness is far older than any wellness trend. It arises from the very fact that humans possess **consciousness**, the capacity to know that we are aware and that this consciousness can be trained, sharpened, and directed. When used well, it becomes a remarkably refined tool for inner clarity and freedom.

At its core, mindfulness is training your mind to stay put. Instead of being dragged back to yesterday's awkward conversation or flung ahead to tomorrow's dentist appointment, the mind learns to rest on one chosen point in the **present moment**. The mind naturally hunts for "juicy" distractions, hopping from thought to thought; mindfulness gently but firmly guides it back, again and again, until attention becomes steady and laser sharp.

In mindfulness meditation, the journey turns inward as you begin to contemplate the mind itself. This focus is not accidental. It is through the mind that you feel emotions, make decisions, act in the world, create possibilities, and relate to others. The mind is the seat of both inspiration and discrimination - where impulses are filtered, values are weighed, and choices are born. To be grounded in a meditative mind is to deepen self-understanding and to respond to life with greater wisdom instead of habit.

The distinctive power of mindfulness meditation lies in the cultivation of **self-awareness**. You can even approach this as an inner scientist. Just as in medicine a new drug is tested against a placebo, to see if it truly has an effect, your spiritual practice can be examined through experience. You can compare periods when you are genuinely aware of sensations, emotions, and thoughts with periods when you are merely going through the motions.

In Sanskrit, the word for this direct, felt experience is *Samvedna*, the living sensation of what is happening within. The real test of meditation is not how beautifully it is described in a book or how noble it sounds as an idea, but whether you can actually feel this inner movement and presence.

History of Mindfulness

In Tibet, a monk named Asangha decided mindfulness needed detailed instructions (bless his organised soul). About 1700 years ago, he laid out a sequence of steps for deepening mindfulness, like a spiritual ladder for the mind. Enter Kamala Sheila, another Buddhist luminary about 1100 years ago, who took Asangha's ideas and turbocharged them in his Sanskrit work "Bhavana Karma", a detailed meditation manual.

Feeling left out by ancient monks. Don't worry; modern science has brought us full circle. John Yates, a neuroscientist and meditation teacher, penned "Mind Illuminated" - a blockbuster in contemplative circles, that translates these centuries-old methods for the wired-and-tired twenty-first-century mind. If you're picturing monks with power tools, you're not far off; this is where spiritual practice meets cognitive science.

In the West, a Vietnamese Buddhist monk, Thich Nhat Hanh played a key role in spreading mindfulness. After being forced to leave Vietnam, he established the Plum Village monastery in France. During the 1970s, he served as a professor at Columbia University. His approach focused on bringing Buddhist principles into daily life.

Later, in 1979, Dr. Jon Kabat-Zinn, a medical doctor and microbiologist, introduced mindfulness to mainstream America. He was instrumental in making meditation a subject of scientific study and clinical relevance, founding the Mindfulness-Based Stress Reduction (MBSR) program at the University of Massachusetts.

What's especially notable is that understanding the mind, habits, and happiness can begin with something as simple as mindful breathing. You do not need to understand everything all at once - instead, mindfulness is cultivated gradually, step by gentle step.

Why Focus on the Breath?

Breath is the anchor of most mindfulness practices, a common thread that unites all living beings. Our breath is ever-present; it is a vital function that connects us to life itself. Through our nose, we inhale oxygen - a necessity for all living creatures, which fuels essential bodily processes via food oxidation and energy creation. When we centre our attention on the breath, we filter out distractions and the mind settles on a single point of focus. This makes respiration intimately linked to our mental and emotional state.

During meditation, when thoughts arise - be they of the past or future, we may respond with craving or aversion. If anger appears, we can notice, "Ah, there is anger." Often, anger or agitation is reflected directly in the breath, making it shallow or fast. As soon as calm returns, breath also naturally regains its smooth, regular rhythm. This sensitive link makes breath a potent indicator of our mental state, and thus an ideal object for mindfulness practice.

The key is simply to attend to the breath. The breath is always available until our last moment, it needs no special effort; it simply is. Meditation does not require us to alter the breath or force anything unnatural. In the stillness of practice, we become aware of each subtle change in the breath, highlighting the impermanence and constant flux of life itself. Don't mix with Pranayama, which has its own benefits.

In this way, the breath also becomes a reminder of the transient nature of existence. As Dr. Paul Kalanithi reflects in his acclaimed book 'When Breath Becomes Air,' the breath marks the boundary between life and death - it is with us one moment, gone the next, leaving only air behind.

Thus, breath meditation grounds us in the present and offers a practice accessible to anyone, anywhere, at any time - regardless of cultural, religious, or personal background. The breath is a secular and universal entry point for developing mindfulness and self-awareness.

Mindful Breath Awareness (MBA)

The practice of Mindful Breath Awareness (MBA) is rooted in Buddhist mindfulness traditions. It is designed to progressively direct your attention from general awareness to highly focused awareness on the breath at the nostrils, facilitating inner calm and insight. Here's a concise breakdown of the four stages involved:

Stage One: Settling into Posture and Present Awareness

- Find a maintainable and relaxed posture: Choose a position that is steady (sthiram), comfortable (sukham), and easy to sustain without strain. You may sit cross-legged, in a chair with feet flat, always keeping your spine straight but not rigid.

- Relax your body: Avoid unnecessary movement, but if an ache or urge arises (like coughing or sneezing), address it gently.

- Close your eyes (optional – half open eye is good): This helps minimise visual distractions and settles the mind.

- Notice the surroundings: Pay gentle attention to ambient sounds and bodily sensations without labelling or following thoughts.

- Non-judgmental observation: Acknowledge any pleasant or unpleasant sensations. Simply note their presence without analysing or reacting.

- Key principle: Remain anchored in present-moment awareness, observing whatever floats through your inner experience without following mental stories or analysis.

Stage Two: Focused Body Awareness

- Transition more deeply: Redirect awareness gradually from general surroundings to the sensations of the physical body - head, neck, chest, hands, waist, and feet.

- Allow other stimuli to recede: Sounds or environmental factors may be noticed but let them fade into the background.

- Centre attention on body sensations: Notice the touch, pressure, temperature, or fullness without judgment.

- Release tension: If you notice stiffness or discomfort, let it go gently through simple awareness.

- Purpose: Make the body itself the focal point of your meditation, cultivating embodied presence and receptivity.

Stage Three: Narrowing Focus to the Breath

- Focus on movement: Notice that in stillness, only the breath moves.

- Direct awareness to breath: Observe the natural flow of inhalation and exhalation – feel the breath at the nose, in the chest, and as the belly expands and contracts.

- Avoid force: Let the breath be as it is, deep or shallow. Do not control or judge.

- Breath as anchor: If thoughts or sensations intrude, let them fade to the background, maintaining gentle focus on the breath.

- Purpose: Develop a deepening connection to the flow of breath, helping the mind become more stable and present.

Stage Four: Attention at the Nostrils (Breath at Nose Tip Awareness)

- Bring attention to the nostrils: Focus on the sensation of air passing at the tip of the nose.

- Do not follow the breath inside or outside: The valuable technique is to keep attention specifically at the nostril area, noticing subtleties like cool or warm air.

- Manage distractions: If thoughts, sensations or feelings arise, let them pass without reaction and gently return focus to the nostrils.

- If attention wanders: Return to previous stages as needed, then gently refocus.

- Actual meditation begins here: Maintaining focused attention at the nostrils is the heart of this practice.

- Count breaths if distracted: Use counting (up to ten and restarting as necessary) as a support to stabilise attention when the mind wanders.

- Purpose: To enter a state of profound awareness and equanimity, observing breath and sensations without judgment or grasping.

Key Techniques:

- Gentle noting: Observe whatever arises - pleasant, unpleasant, neutral sensations or thoughts, without judging or analysing.

- Counting breaths: Useful for overcoming distraction and stabilising attention.

- Returning to focus: When attention drifts, acknowledge it, and return to the breath, celebrating the mini awakening each time.

Core Principles:

- The most important element is attention, how you bring it back gently and non-judgmentally to the breath at the nostrils.

- Through regular practice, you develop equanimity, clarity, and self-awareness.

This approach is universally accessible - anyone, anywhere, from any background or belief, can practice it regularly. Gradually, it cultivates a more balanced and purified mind, in alignment with the wisdom of Buddhist traditions and the principles endorsed by contemporary mindfulness teachers.

As you begin, you'll discover that this foundational practice opens the doorway to deeper self-awareness. Yet, with this simplicity comes an important challenge: distractions naturally arise. Even in the act of focusing on your breath at the nostrils - just breathing in and out, the mind inevitably starts to wander. Recognising and gently working with these distractions is an integral part of the journey.

See Appendix 1: Breath Awareness & Self Focusing Meditation

Guided Meditation - Mindful Breath Awareness (MBA)

What is Self-Awareness?

Breath awareness enhances self-awareness, the mindful understanding of yourself. It means recognising your values, personality, needs, habits, emotions, strengths, and weaknesses. With this insight and a clear vision of who you want to become, you can create effective personal or professional development plans.

Self-awareness involves accurately evaluating your own performance and behaviour and responding appropriately in social situations. This essential skill benefits everyone, from corporate professionals and businesspeople to students, homemakers, and seniors - who aim for professional success, strong relationships, and better health.

Moreover, self-awareness fuels a virtuous cycle that boosts confidence. Being transparent about your strengths allows you to focus energy on your talents, thereby increasing your overall confidence.

Some key benefits of self-awareness include:

1. More empathy toward others
2. Greater compassion
3. Improved listening skills
4. Enhanced critical thinking
5. Better decision-making
6. Stronger leadership abilities
7. Increased self-control
8. Elevated self-confidence
9. Heightened creativity
10. Greater ability to change habits

Who doesn't want success, strong relationships, and improved health? In the following chapters, you will learn how to cultivate calm, relaxation, and focused awareness of yourself and your capabilities.

Building on the foundation of breath awareness, the next vital step is learning to observe the sensations that arise within the body - what the ancient traditions call *Samvedna*. This awareness of bodily sensations anchors our mindfulness in the present moment and deepens our connection to the mind-body interplay.

The Science Behind Observing Sensations (Samvedna)

Acharya Satya Narayan Goenka, a leading teacher of Vipassana meditation, sheds light on this profound process: *"Every contact results in a sensation. This is not philosophy; it is a scientific truth verifiable by all. At every instant, the mind is in contact with matter throughout the body, and with that contact, a sensation arises."*

Cultivating this sensory awareness allows us to move beyond surface distractions and engage with the deeper currents of our physical and mental experiences, paving the way toward true equanimity and insight.

Gautam Buddha discovered why people suffer and how to transcend misery: When defilements like anger arise in the mind, they trigger biochemical flows in the body that increase agitation, feeding the negative state. People can remain stuck in these states for hours, fuelling suffering through habitual reactions.

Goenka highlights that sensations are impermanent, continuously arising and passing away trillions of times per blink, though this impermanence is often hidden from our perception.

Our bodies are not fixed solids but in constant flux. The sensations usually fall into two categories: pleasant or unpleasant. The subconscious mind instantly reacts with craving to pleasant sensations and aversion to unpleasant ones, embedding deep habits.

Some sensory reactions are fleeting; others are deep-rooted and durable. It's crucial not to miss sensations, as mere concentration on breath without awareness of sensations won't lead to purification.

According to Goenka: *"Like respiration, sensations - heat, tension, pressure, vibrations are linked to mental impurities that cause suffering."*

Emotional states like anger produce bodily sensations - heat, sweating, tension that the mind reacts to, perpetuating suffering in a cycle. Often, negative vibrations internally disturb not only ourselves but also those around us.

Observing Sensations in Practice

Breath awareness meditation breaks the barrier so practitioners feel sensations not just superficially but deep within the body. By observing their transient nature, one shifts habitual patterns of mind.

Initially, the mind may be too coarse to perceive deep sensations. But through focused attention, subtle sensations – biochemical currents, vibrations, tingling, tension become noticeable.

Observation starts with the area around the nostrils where breath enters and exits, noting heat, throbbing, or tingling objectively and nonjudgmentally. With continued practice, sensations across the whole body become apparent.

Moving attention systematically from head to foot and back, practitioners become aware of the constant flow of sensations and vibrations. This integrated practice of breath and sensation awareness deepens self-knowledge and cultivates equanimity, setting the foundation for mental purification and lasting peace.

Uncomfortable Sensations

Uncomfortable sensations during meditation are common and arise for several reasons:

- Often, these sensations were already present but unnoticed or suppressed through coping strategies like overeating, drinking, shopping, or excessive social media use. Meditation simply brings them to conscious awareness.

- As meditation deepens, hidden or subconsciously stored pain and discomfort arise into the conscious mind, manifesting as physical sensations.

- Meditation also initiates changes in the brain and ego structure, which can be resisted energetically since our bodies and minds prefer homeostasis.

Common Meditation Discomforts

Feelings of Pressure: Pressure sensations often occur in the chest or forehead, common areas where tension and emotional stress accumulate. These sensations reflect the mind and body processing stress. It is important not to push away or suppress these feelings but to observe them fully with acceptance. Repressing this energy can lead to long-term health issues.

Pain: Pain is universal. Meditation increases awareness of pain that may already exist or arises due to releasing stored tension. Pay attention to pain nonjudgmentally: notice qualities like tingling, numbness, vibration, or whether it pulses or changes. Recognising pain as impermanent helps transform habitual reactive tendencies into calm equanimity. If pain is overwhelming, shifting to breath focus or adjusting posture helps maintain meditation practice.

Uncomfortable Energy: Beginners often feel vague uncomfortable energy – manifesting as agitation, fear, restlessness, or doubt. Underlying this is usually a distinct physical sensation (heaviness, tightness, tingling, coolness, etc.). Viewing this energy with curiosity and without judgment allows it to pass naturally. Recognise, that it will not last forever and does not hold real power over you.

Importance of Breath Awareness and Equanimity

According to Acharya Satya Narayan Goenka, breath-awareness combined with equanimity (non-reactivity) is essential for purifying the mind. Regardless of whether sensations are pleasant or unpleasant, avoid craving or aversion as these reactions breed suffering.

Progress on the meditation path is measured by the equanimity developed, particularly at the level of bodily sensations. Sustaining awareness of sensations without reactive emotion enables deeper purification of mental impurities and balance in daily life. This wisdom grounded in sensation-awareness equips you to act positively and effectively in the world.

Why Practice Mindful Breath Awareness?

- You learn to *live in the present moment* by anchoring awareness in the present reality of the breath entering and leaving the nostrils.

- This meditation purifies the mind by gradually reducing negativities and mental impurities.

- The mind, like software, requires daily nourishment through meditation to be programmed towards health and balance.

- Being attuned to your feelings helps you improve relationships and personal growth, with limitless potential.

Recommended Practice Guidelines

- Best times: Morning upon waking, night before sleep, or half an hour after lunch.

- Duration: 5 minutes is good, 15 minutes excellent, 45 minutes impressive.

- Frequency: Once daily is good; twice or thrice daily is excellent.

- If health issues exist: Practice 15 minutes three times daily for deeper healing.

This foundation leads to greater self-awareness, emotional balance, and physical well-being as meditation becomes part of your daily life.

Chapter Summary

This chapter highlights the practice of observing the **bare breath** - watching your breathing naturally, without altering it. The goal extends beyond concentration, aiming for **mental purification** and releasing inner negativity. Using breath as an anchor helps steady awareness and foster genuine freedom.

Key ideas to carry forward are:

- During meditation, mental defilements like anger, fear, passion, and resentment will naturally surface, creating inner turbulence; this is part of the cleansing process, not a failure.

- Reacting to these sensations with craving or aversion builds tension within and sends ripples of suffering into our relationships and environment.

- Mindfulness trains you to observe sensations **non-reactively**, cultivating **equanimity** – a balanced, poised state that interrupts the cycle of suffering and progressively purifies the heart.

- Early practice often feels uncomfortable or distracted, which actually signals that deeper layers of conditioning are being revealed.

- Avoid mantras, mental commentary, or visual focus in this practice; keep attention gently but firmly on the bare breath.

- Breath awareness roots you in the present moment, supports inner calm, and, over time, strengthens emotional resilience and self-awareness.

- Patience and persistence are essential, as genuine transformation unfolds gradually.

Reflect & Apply

- **Reflect:** Notice how often, in meditation and daily life, you react with craving (clinging) or aversion (resisting). Observe how these reactions immediately affect your inner peace and clarity.

- **Apply:** At the start of each meditation, set a gentle intention to observe the breath exactly as it is. When distractions arise, acknowledge them and calmly return attention to the natural breath.

- **Integrate:** During the day, periodically observe bodily sensations and emotions with curiosity, practising non-reactivity amid everyday challenges.

- **Grow:** Use insights from this mindful observation to recognise your habitual patterns and triggers, and experiment with new, wiser responses.

With consistent practice, this simple yet profound discipline of breath awareness nurtures the discipline, clarity, and equanimity needed to sustain enduring peace and personal fulfilment.

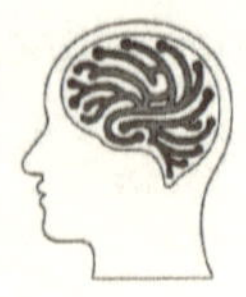

4

Power of Mindful Visualisation

~ Whatever your mind can conceive, you can achieve.

A Transformative Power

Visualisation is often misunderstood as mere daydreaming. In truth, it is the intentional creation of detailed mental pictures - like still photographs or movies, depicting the outcomes you wish to realise. Research, such as the study by Vasquez and Buehler (2007), highlights how elite athletes use visualisation to enhance performance and success. This powerful tool extends beyond sports, helping people overcome illnesses and achieve diverse goals - be it writing a book, earning a promotion, financial independence, dream vacations, weight loss, or skill improvement. Let me share a story.

Turning Dreams into Reality

Brig Rahul (name withheld for privacy), a MindRetreat participant, had long dreamed of running his first half-marathon after retirement but was held back by self-doubt and fear of failure. During our sessions, he learned to use visualisation as a tool, not as fanciful daydreaming, but as a detailed mental rehearsal. Each day, Rahul in his mid-sixties, vividly pictured the morning of the race: waking up refreshed, the cool air on his face, the rhythm of his feet on the pavement, and the triumphant moment crossing the finish line surrounded by cheers.

This daily practice shifted Rahul's mindset. His confidence grew, his training became more focused, and he developed mental resilience to push through fatigue and setbacks. On race day, he calmly tapped into the mental movie he had rehearsed so many times. This presence and preparation carried him through successfully completing the Navy Half-Marathon 2024, a goal he once thought impossible.

Rahul's story demonstrates how visualisation shapes both mind and body, turning a distant goal into a lived reality. Like elite athletes and great achievers, intentional visualisation can help you calm fears, build focus, and manifest your dreams with clarity and conviction.

Meditation and Visualisation

When asked about the gains from meditation, Buddha replied, "Nothing. But I lost anger, anxiety, depression, insecurity, fear of aging and death." Meditation is less about acquiring something new and more about shedding mental burdens, leading to a lighter, freer self in harmony with inner truth. This transformation ignites motivation and inspires personal growth and mental wellness.

Meditation is all about the power of your visualisation. Let's learn a few definitions of the terms we will use in our program. Visualisation and imagination are qualities of creative people that help them be more effective in problem-solving. Let's look at the definition:

- **Visualisation:** Remembering or mentally recreating something seen before.

- **Imagination:** Creating mental images of things unseen, which can evolve into visualisations; crucial for problem-solving, creativity, and manifestation.

You can experience success through visualisation by vividly imagining yourself succeeding - feeling, sensing, and believing you have already achieved your goals. BK Sister Shivani says, *"This positive conviction powers your efforts, making success more likely. Conversely, dwelling on past failures fosters frustration and loss of enthusiasm."* Instead, visualise yourself as someone who has conquered fears and transformed negative habits.

Internal and External Conditions Influence State

Many visualise the actual event, i.e., they create pictures of success in their consciousness. It means they imagine themselves in the moment of victory, feeling the emotions, experiencing the sensations, and visualising they have already achieved their goal. The same principle of visualisation is also used to cure patients from illnesses, including cancer. Patients are taught to visualise their diseased organs or free from diseases and receive healing energy.

You visualise yourself as a person who has already overcome his fears and negative habits. The fears are removed, and the negative habits are transformed.

I will share some of the terms we shall use in this program.

What creates the state we are in?

- **Internal conditions:** Beliefs, values, past experiences shape perceptions and behaviours.

- **External conditions:** Nutrition, breathing, posture, muscle tension, biochemical states affect feelings and energy.

Change involves shifting behaviour (internal condition) and altering feelings via physiological changes (external condition). Affirm to yourself in the present tense ("I am a soul full of powers"), fostering positive transformation and awakening the subconscious. When a human being wants to change something, they usually want to change one or both of these two things:

- How they behave – they change their internal conditions.

- How they feel – They change their external conditions: physiology.

Enhancing Your Visualisation

Exercises tailored to sharpen sensory faculties boost awareness and mental clarity. Ask yourself:

- What mental images arise when thinking about the world or your future?

- Are they clear or vague, positive or negative?

Your imagination shapes your reality. Consistent visualisation work lets you replace negative thought patterns with empowering ones, creating the life you desire. These exercises are designed to sharpen your sensory faculties, leading to heightened awareness and mental clarity.

Sherin Mathews, my colleague and a storyteller from Mumbai says, *"Storytelling, especially before puberty, stimulates imagination, helping children form vivid mental movies that enhance creativity."*

Visualisation primes the mind by creating clear, intentional mental images of the outcomes we desire. Building on this foundation, Self-Focusing Mindful Meditation deepens our ability to anchor attention, cultivate inner calm, and sharpen awareness, essential skills that sustain and empower the visions we hold. Together, these practices unlock your mind's creative potential, transforming not just what you imagine but how fully you live it.

See Appendix 1: Breath Awareness & Self Focusing Meditation

Guided Meditation – Enhance Your Visualisation

Self-Focusing Mindful Meditation

Rooted in ancient Indian wisdom and refined over millennia, these meditations (like Yog Nidra, Vipassana, and Preksha Dhyan) harness the mind's creative potential. Paramhansa Yogananda said, "Our consciousness creates our world, and with proper training, you can develop the ability to shift your mind."

Key tips during practice:

- Notice sensations deeply, observing their impermanence to transform habitual thought patterns.

- Follow guided visualisation and positive affirmations attentively; missing instructions is okay, just return to present awareness.

- Engage all five senses in visualisation to enhance vividness, e.g., feel wind, smell aromas, feel textures.

This foundational work in visualisation and mindful meditation equips you to harness your mind's power creatively and consciously, supporting profound personal transformation and goal achievement.

Instructions to follow during meditation

As you go through this guided exercise, you'll hear a couple of things from me, which I want to explain upfront so there are no surprises. Follow these instructions:

- **First** point: You will be asked to relax your body from the top of your scalp down to your toes. That will take 7–8 minutes, and it will help you sink into a mighty state of physical relaxation. It's fantastic when you come out and feel your body is rejuvenated.

- **Second** point: We will start by saying to feel a tingling sensation, a feeling of vibration in your scalp. How do you do that? Well, imagine someone has placed a warm cloth on your scalp, and imagine what that would feel like. Then, slowly bring that feeling of vibration down to your toes.

- **Third** point: When I say, "*You will next hear my voice after one hour has elapsed at this level,*" I will start speaking in 60 seconds. One hour would not have elapsed in the real world, but in your mind, your subconscious would feel that one hour has just elapsed, and you are being rested and peaceful.

- **Fourth** point: At this level of consciousness, you will also hear me use certain positive statements. Repeat them in your mind.

- **Fifth** point: A positive statement will help you enhance your intuition. This meditation uses positive statements to help bring out different dormant faculties of your mind.

- **Sixth** point: When I say find a comfortable position, don't worry about getting too comfortable; it might make you fall asleep. However, keep your body still. As you go through this exercise, understand that if you feel a light itch or need to readjust your legs, it's perfectly okay to scratch it.

- **Seventh** point: You will be required to project yourself mentally to your ideal place of relaxation. Choose any place and use your imagination or visualisation. It could be your favourite mountain, riverside, or forest you have visited and seen. It could be an imaginary place, like clouds, the bottom of the sea, another planet, whatever. Once you choose, it should not be changed for six to 12 months. Avoid choosing frequently visited places, like a room, market, temple, etc.

- **Eighth** point: In gratitude, when blessing Mother Earth, raise your right hand. Close to your chest, palm facing outward.

The exercise itself will keep you at a deep level of mind. Get ready to enjoy the mind-focusing exercise. Before we start this meditation, please take 5 minutes to empty your bowels, sip water, and relax.

We will begin this exercise with the three-two-one (3-2-1) method. Level 3 is for physical relaxation, level 2 is for mental relaxation, and level 1 is for complete relaxation.

See Appendix 1: Breath Awareness & Self Focusing Meditation

Guided Meditation – Mindful Self Focusing: 3-2-1

This meditation guides you through three levels of relaxation:

- Level 3: Physical relaxation

- Level 2: Mental relaxation

- Level 1: Deep, essential relaxation

Alpha Activator: 3 Finger Anchoring

Achieving something once or twice is not real success; that is coincidence. Genuine success is **repeatable** success, and for that you need a simple, reliable inner system rather than starting from scratch every time.

The Alpha Activator is that system. It is a 3 Finger Anchoring technique that helps you retain and quickly recall a calm, creative, resourceful state – very similar to the Alpha state you experience in meditation, and you can often access it even with eyes open. During meditation, you link this inner state to a small physical trigger: gently bringing three fingers together. Later, whenever you touch those three fingers in the same way, your mind learns to slip back into that Alpha state easily and quickly.

You can use either hand for this activator, preferably the nonworking hand. Your fingers become a discreet reminder that you are now choosing to respond from your higher, centred self.

This is especially powerful for repeated, highimpact situations where honest, fair intentions matter, such as: appearing for an exam or interview, walking into an important business meeting, finding parking in a crowded market, receiving good service during travel and dining, or meeting and handling difficult people. The programming can be done in advance at your convenience.

Over time, the threefinger touch becomes your personal "Alpha switch," taking you straight into your inner kitchen - the subconscious mind, whenever you need it most.

Process - 3 Finger Anchoring

Sit comfortably and close your eyes. You may use either hand for this technique. Your three fingers will serve as a physical reminder to address your challenge, helping you quickly and easily enter your Alpha state - your inner, subconscious mind.

For example, imagine you have an important meeting with your boss.

Before you begin, mentally prepare yourself by locking your three fingers together and bringing them close to your heart. Say quietly to yourself:

"I am going to discuss my new project with my boss. My breathing is calm. My eye contact is confident. My voice is clear and strong. My thoughts flow smoothly and precisely. My presentation will be perfect. I look energetic and positive. I am confident in the best way."

As you approach your boss's door, take a deep breath and gently knock using your three locked fingers. During the meeting, keep your fingers locked. This simple gesture helps you stay focused and connected while expressing your ideas or making points.

The three locked fingers symbolise your access to all inner resources - courage, patience, tolerance, compassion, and more.

If you need to shift focus or cancel a previous programming - perhaps about a project or situation, lock your three fingers again and say to yourself firmly:

"Cancel, cancel, cancel." Then unlock and reprogramme with a new positive affirmation.

This method empowers you to maintain composure, access inner strength, and adapt your mindset intentionally in any situation.

Divine Sweep Meditation

This technique involves rapidly moving attention from the head to toes and back, flowing energy through the body without blocks or blind spots. This intense scanning helps:

- Reduce the power of surfacing emotions linked to memories by observing the accompanying sensations rather than the emotions themselves.

- Accelerate settling of mind by recalling impermanence and sweeping over the body quickly (sometimes in one breath).

During meditation, you may experience a rapid scanning of bodily sensations, moving your attention quickly from head to toe and back. This is often called the *Divine Sweep*. When your mind flows smoothly without blockage or "blind spots," you may feel an unimpeded flow of energy or awareness through the body.

Key Terms:

- Sensations: Feelings or vibrations within the body.

- Subtle sensations: Delicate, faint, or minor bodily feelings.

- Gross sensations: Strong, unpleasant, or significant feelings.

When old memories or emotions arise, they may attempt to overwhelm you due to habitual reactions. To manage this:

- Acknowledge that an emotion or memory has surfaced, but don't delve into its details.

- Shift your focus from the emotion or memory itself to the *sensations* or feelings present in your body.

- Observe these sensations with attention and acceptance, this helps weaken the emotional charge.

- Even if overwhelming, with practice, the duration and intensity of these sensations diminish - eventually rendering emotions, less overpowering.

If the mind wanders excessively or if focusing on body parts like extremities doesn't help:

- Try moving your awareness rapidly through the body from head to toe and back.

- This motion should mimic a fast scan, ideally done within one or two breaths.

- The aim is to sweep away mental blockages and settle the mind by recalling the impermanent nature of sensations ("impermanence").

Practical Tips:

- If no blockages exist, you can glide through the body in one breath; blockages will require multiple breaths, so be patient and don't force it.

- Include your arms in this scanning process, keeping them together to maintain the flow.

- Difficulty moving awareness through the legs is common initially:

  - Practice lying down with legs straight to ease the process.

  - Later, gradually include bending legs as comfort allows.

- Regular practice leads to smoother, more consistent scans.

This method helps cultivate mindfulness of sensations, increasing equanimity and reducing the power of disruptive emotions during meditation.

Overcoming Distractions & Challenges

Distraction and Mindful Responses

During breath awareness, the mind naturally gets pulled by thoughts, memories, sensations, and sounds, so the task is not to fight distraction but to recognise it and return. When you notice you have forgotten the breath or your attention has wandered completely, simply acknowledge this and gently guide your focus back to the sensations at the nostrils, treating each return as a small moment of awakening rather than a failure.

Counting the breath can help stabilise attention when the mind feels scattered: after an in-breath and out-breath, mentally note "one," then continue - "two," "three," and so on up to "ten." Restarting from "one" whenever you lose the count, without self-judgment. The aim is to let counting support awareness, not replace it, so keep it light and natural.

Be alert to the point where it becomes mechanical - psychologists observe that after some repetitions (say, ten or more), counting can run on autopilot while the mind wanders, and whenever you notice this, gently drop back into fresh, mindful contact with the living breath.

Facing the Common Challenges

Many people wonder how to begin meditation or become discouraged when thoughts rush in and disrupt their practice. It's the most common experience: as soon as we close our eyes, our minds fill with a parade of thoughts, making stillness seem impossible.

A second hurdle is trying too hard to force concentration. It's important to remember that concentration is not the goal, but a natural outcome of authentic meditation. Trying to "concentrate" is like trying to fall asleep - the harder you try, the further it seems.

Thoughts, like hearing or sight, are natural. Through meditation, we learn to train the mind - not to silence thoughts by force, but to use thinking in a heightened, creative way. Whenever thoughts arise, simply remind yourself: "I am meditating now." Let those thoughts drift past like clouds in the sky, without resistance or attachment.

Simple Meditation Practice Tips

Building Your Meditation Practice

- A calm and subdued mind is the foundation for meditation.

- As stated in the last verses of Chapter 5 of the Bhagavad Gita, meditation and self-realisation require ongoing practice.

- Begin with ten minutes a day and gradually build up to thirty.

- Consistency will bring ease, and you will recognise your progress naturally.

- Meditate early in the morning when the surroundings are quiet, ideally around 6 am, and after bathing to feel fresh and alert.

- Find a comfortable seated position - on a chair or floor, using mats or cushions as needed. Adjust clothes and posture for comfort. Avoid bed.

Focus on Internal Sounds

- Close your eyes and slow your breathing, listening attentively to its sound.

- Meditation is about maintaining focus. Expect your mind to wander; your task is to notice when it does and gently return to your breath.

- Your mind creates images linked to sounds: hearing a train brings a mental picture of a train, rain evokes rainfall images, etc.

- The goal is to listen to sounds without forming images - cultivating a blank, tranquil mind.

Developing Concentration

- After some time, shift your attention to your heartbeat's sound. You may start to hear faint, continuous sounds, like echoes after a sudden loud noise or ringing bells.

- Maintain focus on these subtle sounds as long as possible, gently bringing your attention back whenever distracted.

Mindful Awareness & Consistent Practice

Awareness & Equanimity

Acharya Satyanarayana Goenka emphasises:

- Awareness combined with equanimity is essential in purifying the mind.

- Reacting with craving or aversion causes suffering; the goal is to develop non-reactivity even amid sensations.

- Equanimity on the level of bodily sensations is the true measure of progress.

- Balanced awareness enables wise, calm decisions beneficial to self and others.

Practice with Consistency & Congruency

To maintain regular meditation practice:

- Create consistency: Carve out daily practice time, starting small and building up.

- Use reminders: Sticky notes or scheduled times.

- Buddy system: Meditate with others for motivation.

- Ease intentions: Adjust goals to maintain engagement without stress.

- Align intention and practice: Ensure your thoughts, attitudes, and beliefs support the goals you pursue.

Swami Satyananda Saraswati notes that practices like Yog Nidra, rooted in ancient traditions, can deeply change the mind and cure ailments by accessing the subconscious.

Choosing the Right Practice

Select meditation techniques aligned with your specific objectives – whether relaxation, healing, creativity, or other goals. Both visualisation and mindfulness tools can be adapted for individual aims.

This comprehensive approach blends – focused meditation, trigger anchoring, rapid body scanning, and mindful equanimity. This fosters lasting mental clarity, resilience, and transformative growth. Regular, congruent practice ensures that meditation becomes a powerful tool for sustained success and wellbeing.

Chapter Summary

This chapter shows how awareness, equanimity, imagination, and meditation are vital for reaching your full potential. Practices like meditation and mindfulness support inner peace and a positive mindset, helping you achieve life goals. Consistency between thoughts, emotions, and actions is essential for lasting change.

Key ideas to carry forward are:

- **Meditation for purification:** Meditation trains you to observe sensations and emotions without reacting, craving, or resisting, gradually calming and purifying the mind while fostering deep inner peace.

- **Power of visualisation:** Vividly imagining your desired outcomes "as if already achieved" engages the subconscious and is widely used by top performers to align belief, motivation, and action.

- **3-2-1 relaxation technique:** Moving through physical relaxation (3), mental relaxation (2), and deep essential relaxation (1) helps release tension, clear mental clutter, and support inner cleansing.

- **Alpha Activator / 3-finger anchoring:** This technique allows you to quickly access calm, resourceful states and pre-programmed responses from meditation sessions whenever needed during the day.

- **Daily consistency:** Even 5–15 minutes of regular meditation can reduce emotional reactivity, improve regulation, and stabilise your inner state over time.

- **Mindset hygiene:** Avoiding negative self-talk, focusing on what you want (rather than what you fear), and actively wishing well for others help maintain a constructive, uplifting inner environment.

Reflect & Apply

Use these prompts to integrate the chapter into daily life:

- **Reflect:** How often do you notice sensations and emotions without judging them? When distractions or negative thoughts arise, do you react automatically or respond with awareness and equanimity?

- **Apply:** Start or deepen your practice using the **3-2-1 relaxation** and **Alpha Activator** techniques to stabilise focus and access calm, centred states throughout the day.

- **Visualise:** Regularly rehearse detailed visualisations of your goals already fulfilled, engaging sight, sound, feeling, even smell and taste, to strengthen belief and enthusiasm.

- **Commit:** Design a realistic meditation routine—time, place, duration—and use reminders, partners, or groups to stay accountable and consistent.

- **Align your mindset:** Check whether your thoughts, words, and actions truly support your goals. Adjust wherever there is misalignment so your inner energy backs your highest aspirations.

With patience and persistence, these practices help you shift from reactive habit to mindful choice, opening a sustained path toward growth, happiness, and authentic success.

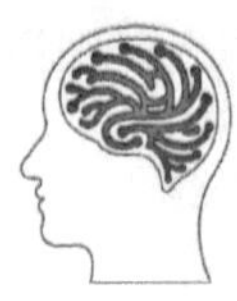

5

Power of Mind

*~ Everything that happens outside of you results
from everything inside your mind.*

Unlocking Your Mind's Hidden Power

Drawing from the integrated understanding of mind, brain, and body as a dynamic system, it is clear that true power lies not just in possessing raw mental capacity, but in how we harness and train our mind's energy. Imagine your brain as a supercomputer brimming with untapped potential, and your mind as the software that must be intentionally programmed (reference Chapter 1). In a world distracted by screens and endless social media scrolls, few consciously engage this incredible inner resource. This chapter invites you to reclaim control through visualisation and affirmations - tools that activate your mind's hidden power and move you from reactive autopilot to deliberate mastery.

Everyday challenges - be it family tensions, unsolicited advice, or unforeseen setbacks, can cloud your clarity and drain your energy. Yet the ultimate choice is yours: to dwell on negativity or to visualise your success and affirm your unstoppable spirit. When adversity strikes, use your mind as a lion uses its focus: zero in, persist, and overcome. To embody this mindset, consider the story of Mel Fisher - the treasure hunter who refused to give up. Have you heard of him?

Legendary Mindset: The Mel Fisher Saga

Mel Fisher - the treasure hunter who dedicated 16 years to uncovering a 17th-century Spanish shipwreck off the Florida coast. A WWII Army veteran and former chicken farmer, Mel's relentless pursuit exemplifies the transformative power of steadfast focus and belief. When asked why he remained loyal through setbacks, one crewmember's response reveals a universal truth about mindset.

He replied, *"Mel just could get everyone excited. Every day, Fisher told himself and the crew, Today's the day …".*

The Mel Fisher Museum was opened in Florida in the 1990s. Mel passed away in 1998. He is a classic example of the ultimate success formula. He had complete mastery and control over his mind. He believed in what he thought. He demonstrated an attitude to accomplish his goal.

Reflections

Words are like ninja stars, they can defend or wound, build alliances or start battles. Be smart with what you say - to others and, most importantly, to yourself. After all, as David J. Schwartz points out in *The Magic of Thinking Big*, success isn't about how heavy your brain is, but how big your thinking is. So, think big, my friend, really big. The key thing to remember is that your mental state has incredible power, and you can control it. You don't have to be at the mercy of whatever comes your way.

Is Your Life Just a Reflection of Your Mind?

Take a moment here, who do you hang with? How's your relationship with your family (and yes, your humble self)? Are you skipping the third samosa… or embracing it with gusto? Your life, from your daily habits to your deepest beliefs, is a mirror of your mental broadcasts. So set your station: Drama channel or Zen paradise? Choice is yours - pick wisely.

Why Focus on This Now?

To level up your life with:

- More personal power and control
- Greater determination and grit
- Richer relationships with real connection
- Sharper clarity and empowered beliefs

- Better health and holistic wellness

Affirmations: Your Mind's Daily Vitamins

Forget the old "time heals all wounds" cliché. Time is just a calendar entry. Your feelings? They live in your mind and only you can heal them. Enter positive affirmations: short, sweet, and powerful mindset hacks you repeat to yourself - ideally when your brain's in that chill Alpha state. These affirmations don't just soothe, they rewire your thinking for resilience and optimism.

Your life is a direct reflection of your thoughts. How and when you engage your mind can create a significant impact. You are in control of your life, and it is your responsibility to make things happen.

It is essential to understand the importance of healing both us and others. While advice can offer support, it does not always lead to true healing. So, what has the power to heal people? It is your energy, your vibrations. Consider the last time you walked into a temple, church, or meditation centre and felt an undeniable sense of peace. Many of us have experienced that uplifting energy. What shifts in those moments? You are connecting with a higher vibration.

See Appendix 4: Affirmations & Manifestations

The Art of Affirmation Writing

Raise Your Frequency, Raise Your Life

This higher vibration influences my mind because I embody a foundation of peace. I confidently declare - 'I feel at peace'. Remember, this higher vibration doesn't solely originate from places of worship. You can cultivate a state of being through positive thoughts, actions, and interactions. You're actively contributing to their healing when you radiate this higher vibration to those around you.

Ever noticed how just walking into a temple or a peaceful garden shifts your mood? That's because you're tuning into higher vibes, the kind that makes stress do a faceplant. Guess what? You're a walking, talking vibe-generating machine. When you project calm and positivity, you don't just raise your energy - you uplift the whole room.

Everyone wants more - better health, stronger relationships, professional success, spiritual connection. But the real win is "holistic wellness" - being physically fit, emotionally balanced, mentally sharp, and spiritually aligned. That's when life feels complete.

ABCD – The Secret Sauce to Excellence

(Inspired by the wisdom of Prabhu Gaur Gopal. Das, a monk with a knack for life coaching)

Want a foolproof recipe for becoming the best version of yourself? Whether you're prepping for exams, climbing the career ladder, or just trying to win at life, this ABCD formula is your game-changer.

A – For Absorption

Absorption is the secret sauce of excellence. It's not just about putting in hours or going through the motions - it's about *being truly present*, fully immersed in what you're doing. Think about Tiger Woods, who famously boiled down his success to three words: practice, practice, practice. But behind that repetition is the magic ingredient - *deep focus*.

Let me share a story that perfectly captures this. Prabhu Gaur Gopal Das, a monk and gifted motivational speaker from ISKCON, once spoke about his visits to a notoriously chaotic medical college hostel. Picture this: the hostel rooms were tiny, cramped, and let's just say, less than pristine. The corridors were littered with flags, clothes hanging everywhere, and the noise was the kind that could make a rock concert feel peaceful.

Yet, in one of these crowded, noisy rooms, sat a student so engrossed in his studies that he seemed to be in his own universe. The music blared through the walls, but this student was unbothered, he didn't hear the noise, he didn't see the chaos. To him, the distractions simply *did not exist*. He was so absorbed that the world around him faded into the background.

That's the power of absorption. It's a state where nothing distracts you, because your mind is laser-focused on mastering your craft.

Remember Mohammad Rafi, the legendary Bollywood singer? He wasn't just talented; he was deeply absorbed in his work. Imagine holding a single note - called *Huaraz*, the lowest on a keyboard and holding it for hours without once flinching or being distracted by life's insistent background noise. His mind was so locked in, so present, that nothing could sway him.

This level of absorption isn't just for musicians or students; it applies to every area of your life. Whether it's your academics, your physical fitness, or your relationships, deep focus and immersion are your best tools for real excellence.

On the other hand, distractions, be it noisy music, social media pings, or chattering coworkers, pull you away from your potential. But the cool part? You control this.

When you practice absorption - when you are *fully present*, you can almost magically shield yourself from distractions. This isn't just good advice for hitting the books; it's essential for thriving anywhere.

Gaur Gopal Das says it simply but powerfully: *"If you want to take your relationships, professional life, academic pursuits, or spiritual journey to the next level, you must nurture the art of absorption."*

Ever found yourself in a conversation where the other person's mind is elsewhere or your own, for that matter? That's the opposite of absorption. Practicing being truly present - *listening with your whole self*, brings warmth, connection, and meaning to your relationships.

So, the next time you sit down to study, work, or even chat with a loved one, remember: ditch the distractions, silence the noise, and immerse yourself fully. Those small changes in your focus can make the difference between good and great.

B – For Believe

What do you really believe about yourself? Can you make it? Will you really do it, come what may? Belief isn't some fluffy, inspirational poster word; it's your rocket fuel for success. Whether you hit the mark or miss it, whether you bounce back or stay down, often comes down to two tiny words: I can or I can't. Need a confidence boost for those big exams (or big life decisions)? Start by focusing on what you *can* do, not what you can't. That shift alone is sometimes all it takes to get unstoppable momentum.

Because here's the deal - people who wait for all the resources to land in their lap usually keep waiting. Winners? They start with whatever's in their pocket, their pantry, or their head.

Meet Mahipal Reddy, the Tomato Tycoon of Telangana (July 2023 – The Hindu) - an ordinary farmer with an extraordinary belief. His journey began humbly, with no money and shattered dreams. The sixteen years old lad, son of a poor farmer, was rejected for jobs because he lacked formal education and connections, he faced the harsh reality many do - doors closing, hopes fading. But instead of surrendering, Mahipal turned to the soil. Farming wasn't just a fallback; it was his calling.

With empty pockets but a heart full of fierce belief, he chose to grow what others overlooked - tomatoes in the off-season. Neighbours doubted; markets sneered. Yet Mahipal's answer was always the same: "I can. I will." Armed with nothing but conviction and relentless hard work, he pioneered irrigation techniques and nurtured his crop against the odds.

Years of toil bore fruit, literally and figuratively. Mahipal had built an empire not through shortcuts, but through the unbreakable power of belief.

His story is a beacon: Life will test your patience, pocket, and pride, but belief? Belief whispers, "Try." And that whisper can move mountains.

That's what belief does. It gets you up when the world says sit down.

Or look at Brian Acton, who wanted a job at Twitter and Facebook and got a letter that said, "No, thanks." Most people would grab the ice cream tub and go back to bed. He started WhatsApp. Facebook later bought it - for $19 billion! The world said "No." His belief said "Yes."

Think of Steve Jobs: booted from the company he *created*, he could've held an epic pity party. Instead, he built Pixar, changed animated movies forever, and got himself, bought back by Apple - the ultimate "plot twist" nobody saw coming. He focused on what he could create next, not what he'd lost.

Here's another favourite: A shoe company sends one guy to a faraway town. He returns in despair, "Can't sell shoes there, nobody wears them!" Another salesman is sent and he returned having sold 2000 pairs of shoes. The MD asked, "How"? The guy said that when he asked the first person, he said nobody wears shoes. The second person also said the same thing. He comes back grinning, "That town is full of *opportunity* – nobody owns shoes yet!" Both saw the same facts. One saw a dead end. The other smelled possibility.

I want to tell you another small story about one magic word: BELIEVE.

Once there was a little boy named Vaibhav Suryavanshi, at 14 he was selected to play IPL for RR in 2025, the youngest player ever in IPL. He is from Bihar. Vaibhav loved to play cricket. But he was not the best batsman or the fastest runner. Many times, he got out early. Sometimes, he even dropped the catch. His friends sometimes laughed and said, "Vaibhav, you will never be a good player."

But Vaibhav had one thing: He believed in himself.

Every morning, Vaibhav woke up and said, "I will play better today!" He practiced every day – his batting, his bowling, his catching.

One day, there was a big match. Vaibhav's team was losing. The coach said, "Vaibhav, your turn. Go and bat." Some friends laughed, but Vaibhav remembered his magic word: Believe!

He went into the ground, took a deep breath, and thought, "I can do it." He took his bat and started playing. First, he missed, but he did not give up. He spoke again in his heart: "I believe!" And then, he hit the next ball – a big four!

He kept believing, kept playing. Slowly, his team got more runs. In the last ball, they needed 2 runs. Vaibhav kept his mind strong, "I believe." The bowler threw the ball, Vaibhav hit it and ran fast! Two runs! His team won because he did not stop believing. In his debut match for RR, he scored a century.

Friends, what do we learn? Sometimes, we fail or make mistakes. Sometimes, others laugh or say, "You can't do it." But if you believe in yourself, practice, and do not give up – you can do wonders! Even big cricket stars were small once. They missed catches, got out for zero, or lost matches. But they believed, practiced, and never gave up.

So next time you are at bat, or you drop a catch, or you bowl a no-ball – don't feel sad. Say to yourself, "I will not give up. I believe I can do better." Try again and again. One day, you will surprise everyone – including yourself!

Remember Vaibhav's word – the magic in your heart, BELIEVE!

That's the power of belief: seeing the silver lining, the opening, the big "Yes" where others see "No entry." People who believe they can't see a problem in every possibility. The believer? Sees possibilities in every problem.

So, remember, B is for "Believe." Wherever you are, whoever you are – start now, start small, start believing. The journey of a thousand miles really does begin with that courageous first step. And the next. And the next.

Let your belief be the wind beneath your feet, the voice in your heart whispering, "Go on – you're made for this."

C – For Company

Who you spend your time with can make or break your dreams. Think of your mind as a rocket, and your friends, family, and mentors as your launch crew. Some will fill your tank with encouragement, check your engines, and keep your spirits fuelled; others might try to steal your fuel, intentionally or unintentionally.

Former President Abdul Kalam's childhood in Rameswaram was humble but rich with such influences. Among his closest friends were Ramanadha Sastry – the son of the high priest of their local temple, Aravindan, and Sivaprakasan. Despite coming from different religious backgrounds, these friendships were forged in mutual respect and support, acting as a positive launch crew for young Kalam's soaring ambitions.

His teachers, too, played crucial roles. Sivasubramanian Iyer, an orthodox Brahmin but a rebel at heart, became a mentor who broke social barriers and encouraged Kalam to dream beyond his small town. And his cousin Shamsuddin helped him in small yet meaningful ways, like catching newspapers during the war to help with sales.

Together, these relationships formed a foundation that helped Kalam fuel his determination, even when society sought to clip his wings. They inspired him to rise above limitations and chase his dreams, transforming a newspaper-selling boy from a modest town into India's Missile Man.

Ask yourself today: Do the people you surround yourself with lift you higher? Or do they clip your wings? Choose your launch crew wisely – they can make all the difference between grounded dreams and soaring success.

Gaur Gopal Das puts it brilliantly: *"Excellence is not just about hard work and self-belief. It's about having the right support team - your family, friends, coaches, and mentors who remind you that you CAN, especially on days you feel you can't."* If you hang around people telling you that you'll never succeed, sometimes you start believing them - not because it's true, but because you've heard it too often.

It's like what Adolf Hitler said (a bit dark, but true): *"If a lie is repeated often enough, it starts to sound like the truth. That's how powerful words and energy are. So, be careful - don't let the "naysayers" and "energy vampires" get a seat at your table. If someone keeps dragging you down, make it a "hello and goodbye" relationship."*

Choose people who spark your ambition, who believe in you even when you forget to believe in yourself. Seek out those who challenge you to grow, laugh with you at mistakes, and remind you that you're capable of greatness - academically, professionally, spiritually, and personally.

Remember the story of Jambavan and Hanuman from the Ramayana? One of my favourite characters in Valmiki Ramayana is Jambavan, the King of Bears in the Hindu scripture. He is supposed to have emerged from the mouth of Brahma when he yawned. He assisted Lord Rama, the 7th avatar of Vishnu, in his quest to save his wife Sita from the rakshasa (demon) King Ravana. The news of Sita's whereabouts was conveyed by a vulture bird called Jatayu. But no one wanted to cross the ocean to rescue Mother Sita. Hanuman and his monkeys were sitting and pondering but unsure of their capabilities to cross the ocean and return. At this point, Jambavan came up to Hanuman and said, "Hanuman, you have the potential to cross the ocean because you were cursed to forget your powers until you were reminded of them by another.

Aware of his divine origin, Jambavan, an intelligent Bear King, began describing Hanuman's true powers to all present. As Jambavan finished his speech, Hanuman, remembering his prowess, stood up and, with a great roar, declared to perform the task. Expanding his body to 50 times its normal height, he sprang forth with immense energy to jump across the ocean. Who is your Jambavan? Who helps you remember the Hanuman that's waiting inside you?

C is for Company: Build your circle wisely. Your company is your silent partner in success—choose well, and you'll find your own ocean-crossing strength.

D – For Determination

Now we reach the secret engine that powers all greatness: determination. Think of the epic saga of Arjuna and the Pandavas. They didn't win every battle in the Mahabharata, far from it! They lost beloved warriors, suffered heartbreak, and faced crushing defeats. Yet, every time they stumbled, Lord Krishna was there, urging them to never give up.

Determination in real life doesn't mean never falling; it means always standing back up, sometimes bloodied, but always braver. It's that fierce inner voice that says, "Not today, defeat", no matter how many times life tries to knock you down.

Let me tell you another story. Before he became India's Missile Man and the nation's beloved President, Abdul Kalam was a boy in Rameswaram selling newspapers door to door. Poverty was his constant companion, and opportunities seemed scarce. Yet, his determination was relentless. Every morning before dawn, he carried stacks of newspapers through narrow streets, driven by a vision far beyond his modest surroundings.

Kalam didn't have a smooth path. He faced obstacles, setbacks, and challenges that could have crushed lesser spirits. But like Arjuna, he never let defeat define him. Instead, his determination propelled him toward the stars - literally and figuratively, turning small steps into giant leaps for the nation.

This is determination, the unyielding courage to rise, again and again, despite the odds. Let me tell you another story, one that shows the power of determination in an ordinary person's life:

There was once a young girl named Usha who dreamed of becoming a great runner. Every day, she practiced running faster and farther. But during a big race, she stumbled and fell. Her knee hurt badly, and some of the other runners laughed at her. Many would have given up. But not Usha. She whispered to herself, "I will get up. I *will* finish this race."

Slowly, with pain and grit, she stood up and kept running. Step by step, she chased the runners ahead. She didn't win that day. But her spirit won. Every time she trained after that, she remembered – 'not the fall', but the courage to rise again.

Years later, this lady P T Usha became India's Olympic medallist in 1964 at Tokyo - not because she was the fastest naturally, but because she refused to quit. Her determination made her strong.

Just like Usha, each one of us faces falls and failures. What matters is that we choose to get up, again and again. That's the power of determination. Remember, Rome wasn't built in a day. Even with absorption, belief, and the right company, excellence takes time. It doesn't happen overnight. Patience and perseverance are your allies. You cannot get there straight away, but step by step, with grit and courage, you *will* reach your goal.

Chapter Summary

Excellence requires time and consistent mental discipline. Even with techniques like visualisation, affirmations, and high energy, patience and resilience are essential. The ABCD formula provides a straightforward guide to using your mind effectively for success.

Key ideas to carry forward are:

- **A – Absorption:** Immerse yourself fully in your practice. Mastery comes from focused, repeated engagement, not occasional effort.

- **B – Believe:** Cultivate unwavering faith in your potential. Direct attention to what you *can* do rather than what you can't and let belief fuel persistent action.

- **C – Company:** Surround yourself with people, environments, and content that uplift and stretch you; your mental "ecosystem" either amplifies or drains your power.

- **D – Determination:** Develop grit and resilience. Lasting success demands patience, perseverance, and the refusal to quit when circumstances get tough.

- **Thoughts → Beliefs → Future:** Your thoughts and words shape your beliefs, and those beliefs quietly create your future outcomes.

Reflect & Apply

Use these prompts to turn the ABCD formula into a living practice:

- **Pause and reflect:** Where have you handed your power to circumstances or other people? What is one step you can take today to reclaim that power?

- **Daily affirmation:** Each morning, declare, "I am capable, focused, and determined," and visualise yourself following through.

- **Audit your company:** Honestly assess whether the people and influences around you help you rise. Choose to spend more time with those who inspire your best self.

- **Reframe setbacks:** Recall moments when you bounced back stronger. Let these memories remind you that resilience is your superpower, not your exception.

- **Mind your words:** Listen to your self-talk. Replace criticism and doubt with language that reinforces your potential, worth, and commitment.

Treat this framework as a weekly check-in inside **THE MIND KITCHEN**, steadily nurturing your mind's power to create the life you truly desire.

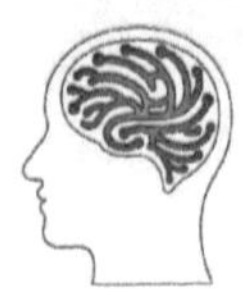

6

Power of Big Thinking

~ Whether you think you can or think you can't – you're right.

Your Power Is Your Choice

Our thoughts shape the world around us, especially in relationships. If we hold hurt or anger in our minds but speak kind words, conflicting energies confuse the connection. If we ignore our inner thoughts, we may unknowingly judge or blame others, creating invisible walls. That's why sometimes, despite our best efforts to be friendly, relationships don't flourish.

The secret? Focus your thoughts on others' goodness and pure intentions. When your heart thinks positively about someone, your words and actions naturally follow, strengthening your bond effortlessly.

The biggest lesson is this: Success begins when you take 100% responsibility for your thoughts, attitudes, and beliefs. Nothing changes unless we change our minds first. Becoming aware of your thoughts reveals your hidden beliefs and actions. This awareness is your steering wheel, you hold the power to guide your life in any direction.

Start right now by embracing the idea that "life is too short to think small," as the great philosopher Disraeli said.

Let me share something inspiring I witnessed years ago during a sales review at Gold Star Jewellery in Mumbai.

The Magic of Big Thinking

Several years ago, I witnessed an exceptionally impressive sales review meeting at Gold Star Jewellery in Mumbai. The CEO was tremendously excited.

He wanted to drive home a point. He had with him on the platform the leading representative in the organisation, a very ordinary but smart-looking fellow who earned for the company a little under Rs 30,00,000 in the year just ended. The earnings of other sales representatives averaged Rs 6,00,000 each. Saumya was not born into wealth or privilege. She was average, just like many of us, but she achieved extraordinary success because she dared to think big.

The Chief Executive challenged the group. He said, "I want you to look at Saumya. Look at her! Now, what's Saumya got that the rest of you haven't? Saumya earned five times the average, but is Saumya five times smarter? No, not according to our personnel tests and records. They show she's about average in this department."

'And did Saumya work five times harder than you fellows? She took more time off than most of you.

"Did Saumya have a better territory? Again, I've got to say no. The accounts averaged about the same. Did Saumya have more education? Better health? Again, no. Saumya is about as average as an average guy could be, except for one thing."

"The difference between Saumya and the rest of you," said the CEO, "is that Saumya thought five times bigger."

Today, Dr. Saumya Badgaiyan Dutta holds a PhD and is respected far and wide – all because she dared to think big.

Reflections

Success, whether in bank accounts, happiness, or peace, depends on the size of your thinking. But many don't think big because their environment pulls them down with small-minded beliefs. Then, as Head of the Training Centre and L&D in Gold Star Jewellery, I proceeded to show that success is determined not so much by the size of one's brain as by the size of one's thinking.

Every moment, you decide how to think and respond. When you blame others, you stay stuck. When you take responsibility, you gain strength. Look for mentors, improve your skills, forgive those who hurt you, these are the ingredients for your success recipe.

Just remember, *doing nothing is still a choice.* The secret is to act, toward goals that bring you joy and abundance. Only you have the power to do that.

Mind Centres on Created Image

The Power of Your Words

Your thoughts create your reality. Believing you can succeed equips you to control your life, face challenges, and bounce back from failures.

But fearing failure and believing you can't? That's a self-fulfilling prophecy.

You manifest your life every day:

- Feel hungry → food appears

- Want to travel → find the right train

- Believe you'll sit → you find a chair

- But you don't think so about doubling your income; it doesn't.

- But you don't believe in having good relationships; it doesn't.

- But if you don't believe in having good health, you remain sick.

Yet, many hesitate to believe in bigger things - like achieving great success, health, or relationships. And because of this doubt, those don't manifest.

How Do We Usually Think and Talk?

Most of us run an invisible commentary in our heads that is framed around what we don't want:

- I don't want to be sick.

- I don't want to be unhappy.

- I don't want to lose money.

- I don't want my marriage to fall apart.

- I don't want my business to fail.

On the surface this sounds sensible, even "positive." After all, you are clearly rejecting what you don't like. But the mind works in images, not in grammar. It does not latch on to the word "don't"; it latches on to "sick," "unhappy," "lose money," "fail." Each time you repeat such a sentence, you are **unintentionally** strengthening the very picture you wish to avoid.

Think of it this way: if a doctor spoke only about illness - symptoms, complications, worstcase scenarios - patients would leave with their attention glued to disease, not health. In the same way, when our self-talk is dominated by problems, our inner focus stays locked on those problems, even when we sincerely want the opposite.

Now notice how a simple shift changes the inner movie. When you say, "I am taking my child to school," you are not just "dropping the kid off"; you create an image of care, responsibility, and connection. Years ago, founder-educationist Chatarbhujbhai Narsee explained this nuance to parents of newly admitted children at Jamnabai Narsee School in Mumbai, and it stayed with me. A small change in words created a very different feeling in the room.

This is the deeper principle behind Wayne Dyer's line: when you change the way you look at things, the things you look at begin to change. By choosing words that paint the picture you actually want, you gently start retraining your mind and your life, to move in that direction.

Personally, I stopped talking about what I lack long ago and started focusing on creating what I desire. It's a simple but powerful habit. Remember the words of David J. Schwartz, author of *The Magic of Thinking Big:* "Success depends not on the size of your brain but on the size of your thinking."

Start today. Your mind is the kitchen, and thinking big is the secret recipe for a delicious life with great relationships.

Build Relationships with Family and Friends

Focus On the Goodness in Others

Today, many of us try hard to keep our loved ones happy - buying gifts, taking trips, dining out often. Yet sometimes, despite these efforts, relationships seem to weaken.

Why? Because relationships are built not just by words or actions, but primarily through our thoughts about others.

Think about it: what picture do you create in your mind when you think about someone? If your thoughts carry pain or anger, even sweet words can produce conflicting energy that weakens your connection. When we judge or blame people unknowingly, we send out negative vibes too. That's why despite trying hard, some relationships struggle.

The key is to focus on the goodness in others. When your thoughts about someone are pure and caring, your words and actions naturally follow, strengthening the relationship effortlessly.

Try this simple yet powerful meditation affirmation:

- *I have perfect relationships. Every thought I have for others is a blessing.*

- *I am a pure being. I think good and bless everyone in my relationships.*

Affirm these thoughts during meditation, when your subconscious mind is most receptive.

Programming your mind this way allows your love, tolerance, and compassion to grow, enriching your connections. By the way, words like sympathy, empathy, and compassion are commonly used. What do you understand by "Sympathy…? empathy…? or compassion…?" I am sharing some advice to help you learn and understand their meaning.

Compassion: The Heart of Relationships

Especially nowadays, with more screen time and less face-to-face, it's vital to build compassion - the ability to deeply understand and support others.

You might have heard words like sympathy, empathy, and compassion. In everything that we do, remember the power of words. For example:

- Sympathy looks in and says, "I'm sorry."

- *Compassion goes in and says, "I'm with you. "*

- Sympathy looks in and says, "I would like to help."

- *Compassion says, "I am here to help."*

- Sympathy says, "I wish I could carry your burden."

- *Compassion says, "Cast your burden on me."*

- Empathy says, "I can understand your rejection in the interview."

- *Compassion says, "I will help you master interview technics."*

Compassion is more than feeling - it's action, a choice to support others lovingly, especially when they struggle.

How to Cultivate Compassion

Here are practical ways to practice compassion daily:

- **Work for the Greater Good.** Do your bit to help the world - small acts of kindness in schools, homes, markets all contribute. Even small help can mean the world to someone. Helping others also nourishes your own heart.

- **Listen Deeply.** When someone is upset, offer a listening ear without judgment or advice. Sometimes, that's the greatest gift.

- **Practice Loving-Kindness Meditation.** Send goodwill in your thoughts to family, friends, and even those difficult to love. This trains your heart to be more open.

- **Take Care of Yourself.** True compassion includes caring for your own well-being. Avoid burnout by being kind to yourself too.

Chapter Summary

This chapter examines the substantial impact of adopting expansive perspectives, detailing how one's thoughts influence key domains such as relationships, health, achievement, and overall well-being. When internal beliefs are consistent with verbal communication, they can produce a unified energy that enhances connections and creates new opportunities; conversely, negativity or inconsistency may subtly undermine outcomes and interactions. A primary conclusion is that success is predicated upon assuming full responsibility for one's thoughts, attitudes, and convictions.

Key ideas to carry forward are:

- **Thoughts build reality:** The quality of your thoughts sets the foundation for what you experience; believing you can succeed equips you to act, persist, and bounce back from failure.

- **From "don't want" to "want":** Most people think in terms of what they fear or wish to avoid. Shifting statements like "I don't want to be sick" to "I am healthy and strong" aligns your focus with what you wish to create.

- **Programming the mind:** Positive affirmations, especially used in calm or meditative states, help reprogram the subconscious for love, abundance, and harmonious relationships.

- **Embrace compassion:** Thinking big is not just about personal gain; it includes expanding your heart to support, uplift, and act kindly toward others.

- **Choose your mental diet:** Just as physical health depends on what you eat, mental health depends on what you consistently think, watch, read, and say.

- **Take full responsibility:** Blaming others keeps you stuck; choosing your responses and mindset puts you back in the driver's seat of your life.

Reflect & Apply

Use these prompts to translate the chapter into daily practice:

- **Assess your thoughts:** Notice the "mental movies" you play about yourself and others. Are they hopeful and expansive, or critical and fearful?

- **Practise positive affirmations:** Write and repeat affirmations focused on what you *do* want, such as "I am surrounded by love" or "My relationships are harmonious and supportive."

- **Cultivate compassion daily:**
  - Show small acts of kindness and understanding.
  - Listen fully without interrupting or judging.
  - Forgive past hurts and let go of grudges that burden your heart.

- **Commit to change:** Each day, make one conscious shift in your language - from complaint to possibility, from blame to responsibility.

- **Meditate regularly:** Use meditation to anchor pure, loving thoughts and to impress your intentions deeply into the subconscious mind.

This chapter invites you to **think bigger, love deeper, and own your inner world**, so you can consciously create the relationships and life you truly desire.

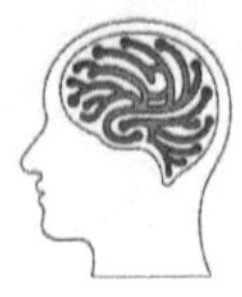

7

Power of Great Attitude

~ The difference between a rich and a poor nation is the people's attitude.

What Is Attitude?

We often marvel at the talent of sports stars, musicians, and artists, thinking, "Wow, I wish I had that skill." But many confuse excellence with skill alone. In reality, talent is only part of the puzzle. Beyond a certain point, skill without the right attitude becomes almost useless. What truly makes a difference is what you do with your talent. And that "what" is driven by attitude - far more than skill itself.

So, what exactly is attitude? It's your response to the people and circumstances around you, whether positive or negative. Your attitude reflects the way you use your ideas, values, beliefs, and perceptions to filter your experiences.

Ultimately, what defines your life is how you manage setbacks and challenges. Let me share my story.

Attitude to Accomplish

At 19, I joined the Indian Naval Academy, then in Cochin (now Kochi) as a cadet. I came prepared, knowing from family history what tough training was like. But the reality was beyond my imagination - harder and more demanding than anything I expected.

Just three days in, on a Sunday, we faced a gruelling 12 km cross-country run around Willingdon Island. No one was allowed to quit or claim injury. Cadets were pushed, even kicked, to keep going.

Reflections

Those who finished, including me - weren't the fastest or the strongest, but we all shared one key quality: a great attitude to accomplish the task.

Charles Swindoll, a well-known Christian pastor and author, wisely said: *"The longer I live, the more I realise the impact of attitude on life. It is more important than facts, education, money, what people do or say, or success and failure. Attitude will make or break your company, your home, and your relationships."*

Put simply, every reaction you make reveals your attitude.

Stories of Responsibility and Precision from Indian Armed Forces

The medics of the defence forces in India and any nation have the most challenging tasks thrown at them. The soldiers with gunshots, injured severely, are evacuated to the base military hospital at Pathankot from Siachen. During Kargil war in 1999, the Doctors and the staff would say confidently: *"If you bring a soldier here, we shall make sure that he goes back to the front"*. It is an attitude of responsibility, integrity, ethics, and, above all, love for the work they do.

Have you seen the Republic Day parade on Kartavya Path in Delhi? Live or on television? Many things happen and are fine-tuned and coordinated in precise 90 minutes. Just 90 minutes. It is all about an attitude of precision. The most fascinating part is the fly-past by 40 aircraft of the Air Force. Taking off from different airfields in India and flying over the Raj Path, now rechristened as Kartavya Path. Never one aircraft got a second late. It is about the pilots' attitude to do their duty with precision.

Why does precision matter so much? Because in war, anything less can mean the nation's fall. In business, a lapse can mean lost deals. In families, it can damage relationships. For students, it can mean lost opportunities. The value of attitude flows through every part of life - from the battlefield to boardrooms, from classrooms to homes.

Prabhu Gaur Gopal Das says: *"Work on your attitude every day. Whether it's trimming a beard or dressing neatly, small things show your mindset. People grow great by valuing the little things."*

Does Attitude Truly Matter Most?

Look at some nations: India and Egypt have ancient civilisations stretching back thousands of years but still face many challenges. Meanwhile, countries like Canada, Australia, and New Zealand were relatively young 150 years ago - yet today, they are prosperous and developed.

The real difference between nations isn't age or natural resources. Japan, despite its mountainous terrain and limited arable land, is still one of the world's largest economies and is projected to rank fifth by nominal GDP in 2025. Germany, powered by precision, discipline, and innovation, holds the position of the world's thirdlargest economy. India is now projected to reach a GDP of about USD 4.19 trillion in 2026, overtaking Japan to become the fourthlargest economy in the world according to IMF estimates.

Switzerland doesn't grow cocoa, yet it's famed for exquisite chocolate and a worldclass banking system. South Korea, with scarce natural resources, sits at the forefront of shipbuilding and electronics.

These contrasts can't be explained by race or raw intelligence - many migrants actually become more productive when they move to such countries and plug into a different ecosystem. The real differentiator is attitude: a mindset shaped over generations by education, ethics, and everyday culture. It is this collective way of thinking - about work, time, trust, and responsibility, that quietly compounds into national prosperity.

What Defines This Winning Attitude?

Look closely at high-performing individuals from armed forces or citizens in well-governed, prosperous countries and a pattern emerges. Most of them live by a quiet but powerful code:

- Ethics: Choosing honesty and fairness, even when shortcuts tempt.

- Integrity: Doing the right thing consistently, not just when it is convenient.

- Responsibility: Owning decisions, results, and mistakes.

- Respect: Treating people and public spaces with genuine regard.

- Punctuality: Honouring time - yours and everyone else's.

- Quality and productivity: Wanting work to be not just done but done well.

- Lawfulness: Following rules even when there is no fear of being caught.

- Love of work: Taking pride in contribution, not just in compensation.

- Savings: Using money and resources wisely, with tomorrow in mind.

- Authenticity: Being truthful, not performing a role for approval.

In many poorer societies, only a minority consistently lives by this code. The gap is not in talent or resources but in attitude - the willingness to embody these values in daily life. As has often been observed in our public discourse, poverty is less about scarcity of minerals or land and more about scarcity of mindset.

We stay stuck when we exploit loopholes, look the other way, and say, "Chalta hai, let it be." Real change begins when more of us quietly decide, "Let it not happen on my watch." When that inner switch flips from passive acceptance to active responsibility, growth follows - first in individuals, then in institutions, and finally in the nation.

Progress depends more on a positive, proactive attitude than on resources, disasters, external threats, or luck.

Attitude is the True Measure of Excellence

You may have noticed that even the most talented people don't always achieve what they're capable of. Why? Because talent alone isn't enough, what really counts is how you respond when you face obstacles.

Harsha Bhogle, the renowned cricket commentator, pointed out an important truth: *"Take Vinod Kambli - a dazzlingly talented cricketer who burst onto the Test scene in 1993 with jaw-dropping performances, including multiple double centuries, only to see his international career fade away by 1995."*

Despite his immense skill and a phenomenal first year averaging over 100, Kambli's attitude let him down. At the highest level, everyone has talent; what separates the truly successful is attitude - the grit, discipline, and resilience that help you weather the storms and push through challenges. Talent may open the first few doors, but it's attitude that carries you through the last one.

Talent might open the first door or the second, but it won't open the last. To reach that final door, you need a winning attitude – a mindset ready to learn, adapt, and persist.

Recently, I encountered two young women – one, a software engineer with great academic results struggling to find placement: another, my mentee, having trouble after a breakup. Both lacked the attitude to reason through their setbacks and make wise decisions. Success doesn't always favour the highest achievers but those with the strongest attitude.

Everyone Matters

Let me share another story with you from my Naval Academy days. During my first month at Naval Academy, then at Kochi, the Chief Instructor (CI) gave the cadets a pop quiz. Cadet Rajan (name changed) was a conscientious student and had breezed through the questions until he read the last one: "What is the first name of the woman who cleans your classroom?" Indeed, this was some joke. He had seen the cleaning woman several times. She was tall, well-built, dark-haired, and in her 30s, but how would he know her name? He handed in his paper, leaving the last question blank.

Just before class ended, one cadet asked if the last question would count toward the quiz grade. The instructor explained: "You'll meet many people in life. Each one matters and deserves your attention, even if all you do is smile and say 'hello'." Rajan never forgot that lesson and learned her cleaner's name: Jaya.

Your attitude determines who and what you value. Every reaction you make reflects your attitude. Your words, behaviour, and feelings reveal your inner state – your hopes, fears, and mindset. While you can't control everything, you can control your attitude. This one string determines how you navigate life's challenges and how your energy influences those around you. The most significant resistance comes from our habits. When you try to change, you will fail. Don't give up!

Never Give Up

There was a man in Britain. Studying at Harrow School. Practically, most prime ministers of England came from there. He had difficulty speaking

English, the British boy. Difficulty understanding English grammar. He could not pronounce it correctly. He never gave up. Later, he was called to speak at Oxford University, where all those guys were doing majors in English. This man walked into the auditorium. They applauded, welcoming him. He approached the podium and waited for the applause to die. He spoke three words. He repeated those three words three times. That was his speech. He picked up his cane and walked out of the auditorium. The audience was clapping 100 times louder. This was the former Prime Minister of England, Sir Winston Churchill. Do you know what Winston Churchill's speech was? He repeated three words – 'Never Give Up'. Second time, 'Never Give Up', and third time again, 'Never Give Up'. Remember, the habits will drag you down.

This is a big mantra. The habits will not allow you to do small things right. There was a guy who broke his jaw three times. The dentist suggested doing a jaw surgery. They wanted to pull out his entire jaw. Can you imagine that surgery? If the jaw is not aligned correctly, then he will be in terrible pain. This man wanted to be a Hollywood star. He was rejected hundreds of times for a misaligned jaw. He never gave up. He is a popular Hollywood star Sylvester Stallone.

There was a lady who got spinal cancer in 1999. Her husband, Maj Bikram Singh Malik, was fighting the Kargil war then. The doctors in the military hospital did three surgeries on her spine. She had 183 stitches. During the surgery, she became paralysed from the waist down. A person with paraplegia. She couldn't sit. She decided to explore. She started trying Javelin throw. Swimming. Shot put. At 31, she won 53 national gold medals and 35 international medals. In 2012, she received the Arjun Award from President Pranab Mukherjee at 42. She also won a silver medal in 2016 at the Rio Paralympics when she was 46. She is Deepa Malik. She was conferred Padma Shri in 2017.

"How can we give up?" Deepa Malik says, "Life is not over. Disability is only a state of mind."

Greatness is not born in comfort; it is forged in pain, setbacks, and quiet comebacks. Has anyone broken his jaw? Has anyone got 183 stitches? Has anyone got spinal cancer? How many times when they decided to change, they were pulled down?

As Admiral Arun Prakash, the Chief of Naval Staff (2004-06), once told a passingout batch of young cadets at the National Defence Academy, greatness is not the absence of failure; it is the refusal to surrender when you fall. True attitude is that inner voice which says, "I will stand up again," no matter how many times the world expects you to stay down.

Change takes time and old habits resist - so be patient and persistent.

Habits Die Hard

During my college days at Jaipur, there was a football match between two collage teams – Maharajas College of Science and Rajasthan College of Arts. Suddenly, our team's goalkeeper fell ill and they couldn't find a replacement. While desperately searching, our team captain, Anand Singh Junia noticed a man loading watermelons into a truck. The man expertly caught every flying melon and placed them precisely in the storage area. The captain thought, "That guy can catch anything - even a ball!"

The final match was a draw. Both teams are equal in goals. Finally, during penalty kicks, the opponent team captain kicked the ball. Wherever the ball came from, the goalkeeper grabbed every ball and put it inside the goalpost. The better team lost the match. That's what are the habits. The goalkeeper held that rubber ball like a watermelon in his hand and shoved it into the goal.

Small Habits, Big Impact: The Five Wheels of Your Life

Real, lasting change doesn't happen overnight. Often, it's the small, consistent habits that quietly shape our destiny - sometimes working for us, sometimes holding us back. To understand how these habits influence your life, think of your life as a car supported by five crucial wheels:

- **First Wheel: Personal Life** - Your passions, hobbies, and self-care practices, fuel your inner happiness and energy.

- **Second Wheel: Family Life** - Relationships with your spouse, children, and close family members provide emotional grounding and support.

- **Third Wheel: Professional or Academic Life** - Your career or studies build your skills, reputation, and financial stability.

- **Fourth Wheel: Social Life** - Friendships and community connections nurture your sense of belonging and joy.

- **Fifth Wheel: Spiritual Life** - Your inner compass – attitudes, values, and beliefs guide you through uncertainty and challenges.

Not all problems you face have easy solutions. Some circumstances are outside your control. But no matter what, never neglect your personal growth and attitude. That is your Fifth Wheel. They are your greatest sources of strength and empowerment, helping you steer your life with confidence.

By nurturing each of these wheels with positive habits and a resilient attitude, you maintain balance and forward momentum - driving your life toward greater fulfilment and success.

I believe there's one thing you should always focus on: cultivating a great attitude. When your attitude is right, success and achievements naturally follow.

Cultivate a Great Attitude

Character Over Clothing

Once, Swami Vivekananda was in London, dressed in his traditional robes. An English gentleman approached him and said, "Why don't you dress like a gentleman?" Smiling wisely, Swami Vivekananda replied, "In your country, a tailor makes a gentleman, but in my country, character makes a gentleman." He reminded everyone that true dignity and respect come not from what we wear, but from the choices we make and the values we uphold.

Building Your World from Within

Let me share a quick story from my family. One evening, my son Nakuul was trying to watch a football game on TV, but his four-year-old son, Sufi, kept buzzing around, restless and chatty. To keep him occupied, Nakuul handed him a jigsaw puzzle of the world map, expecting it to take a good hour. Astonishingly, Sufi finished the puzzle in minutes. Surprised, Nakuul asked, "How did you do it so fast?" With a grin, Sufi replied, "Easy! On the back was a picture of a man. I just put the man together." Then the whole world fell into place.

This simple moment holds a powerful lesson: before trying to fix the world, put yourself together first. Attitude starts from within.

What's Inside Makes You Rise

Here's another delightful story from my family stable: one day, my grandson Sufi approached a balloon seller whose cart was bursting with floating balloons in every colour of the rainbow. Sufi, ever the curious mind, asked, "Will the red balloon fly? The balloon seller said, "Yes".

Sufi persisted, what about the blue one? Or the yellow?" The seller, a bit exasperated, laughed and said, "Darling, it's not the colour of the balloon that makes it soar, it's what's inside that counts."

The lesson is simple yet powerful: it's not outward appearances - skin colour, clothing, or gadgets that determine how high we go in life. It's what's inside us that matters most. And what fills us, more than anything, is our attitude.

Mastery Behind the Moments

Consider the legendary Pablo Picasso. One day, a woman approached him and asked for a quick sketch. Picasso obliged, creating a striking portrait in just 30 seconds, then said, "That will be $30,000." The woman gasped, "But it only took you half a minute!" Picasso smiled and replied, "Madam, it took me 30 years to be able to do this in 30 seconds." True greatness isn't about speed - it's about years of preparation, dedication, with the right attitude.

The Tale of the Holey Socks: A Lesson in Attitude

How many of us have ever slipped on a pair of socks with a hole or two? Now, if you notice a hole, but you don't toss the socks aside, it usually means you value your money and that's a sign of a great attitude. Starting with something as small as a scuffed-up pair of socks, this attitude of appreciation grows. It leads you to value your teachers, respect your colleagues, cherish your work, and be grateful for every opportunity life offers.

But this is the tricky part - some folks wear socks with holes not because they value them, but because the holes hide inside their shoes where no one else can see. Their motto? "No one's watching, so who cares?" That mindset reveals a poor attitude: doing the right thing only when in the spotlight but slacking off when unobserved. People who live this way tend to need constant supervision, reminders, or even worse - a hovering parent to stay on track, always waiting for "someone to watch."

The real magic happens when you adopt an *inner* discipline - the kind of attitude that holds you accountable even when nobody's looking. That's how greatness is cultivated, starting quite literally from the soles of your feet. The above two acts are similar but intentions were different.

Excellence When No One Is Looking

A sculptor was painstakingly shaping a marble statue when a visitor stepped into his workshop. Amazed, the visitor said, "You're a genius - this is a masterpiece." As he wandered around, he noticed another statue, almost identical, pushed into a corner. "So, you got two orders for the same piece?" he joked.

The sculptor smiled and shook his head. "No. That one failed my test."

"What's wrong with it?"

"There's a tiny scratch on the nose," he replied.

The visitor frowned. "But it's going to be placed high up, right?"

"About 20 feet on a pillar."

"At that height, who will ever see a scratch that small?"

The sculptor's answer was simple and quiet: "No one else may see it. But I will and so will God. If I accept this, I'll always know I chose halfhearted work over my best."

That quiet refusal to compromise, even when no one is watching, is the essence of true excellence and the hallmark of a great attitude.

Power Of Choice

Wouldn't You Rather Soar Like an Eagle Than Quack Like a Duck?

Let me tell you a story. During a recent trip, because my job has me bouncing around quite a bit, I found myself waiting at the airport in Udaipur - popular tourist destination and my native place. The queue was long, but then this cab pulled up, gleaming like it had just won a car wash contest. The driver stepped out, sharp as a tack in a crisp white shirt, black tie, and freshly pressed trousers. He popped the dickey, gave me a nod, "Sir, that's two bags," and before I could even settle in, handed me a laminated card.

Curious, I glanced down. It said: "Khama Ghani (salutation), I'm Bhawani Singh, your driver. Here's my mission statement." Mission what? I was intrigued.

Bhawani, full of pride, explained, "My mission is to get you to your destination the quickest, safest, and cheapest way, all with a friendly smile." Now, that's not the usual "Just hop in" cabbie story!

Inside, his cab was spotless. I'm talking showroom clean: no stray wrappers, no suspicious smells, no sticky seats. Impressive.

As we pulled away, Bhawani asked, "Coffee? I have regular and decaf." I joked, "Nah, just give me a soda."

"No problem," he smiled, "I've got Diet Coke, regular Coke, lassi, and orange juice." Surprise! I went for the lassi, it's Udaipur after all.

Then, just as you think he's done, Bhawani whips out a menu of newspapers and a list of radio stations with their playlists. The air conditioning was perfectly tuned, and he offered some pro tips on the best route for the time of day.

Naturally, I asked, "Bhawani, have you always been this… um, extraordinary?"

He chuckled, "Not really. In my first five years driving, I was your typical grumpy cabbie. Complaining, yawning, the lot. Then, one day, I heard about something called the POWER OF CHOICE."

Bhawani's eyes sparkled. "What's that about?", I asked.

He said, "You can choose to be a duck or an eagle. Ducks wake up already expecting a bad day - they quack, complain, and flail around. Eagles? They soar above the chaos, majestic and calm. I chose to soar.

And soar he did. Slowly at first, but eventually Bhawani transformed his service bit by bit. Other drivers' cabs were dirty, drivers grumbled, passengers scowled. Bhawani flipped the script - with cleaner car, warmer smiles, and thoughtful service.

"How's business?"

"I doubled my income last year," Bhawani grinned, "and this year? I'm aiming to quadruple it. Customers call me directly now." The guy chose to stop quacking and start soaring.

Reflections

Every day you pick your destination. Success isn't accidental, it's the result of the attitude you bring. So, what will you choose: to quack with the ducks or soar with the eagles?

Now, how many of you hit the snooze button in the morning? Remember, it's not about the alarm, it's about your choice you make and the attitude you wear. If you don't respect your own commitments, your day, studies, and career will suffer. Greatness lies in the small, consistent habits you nurture daily.

Chapter Summary

This chapter argues that attitude drives excellence and success more than talent or skill. It influences how we handle pressure, people, and setbacks, appearing in both major operations and daily routines. Examples from the Indian Armed Forces, Churchill, Stallone, and Deepa Malik illustrate that greatness stems from perseverance, integrity, and attention to detail.

Key ideas to carry forward are:

- **Attitude > Talent:** Skill can open doors, but attitude decides whether you walk through and stay there. The right mindset is critical for long-term success.

- **Every action reflects attitude:** Tiny behaviours - like punctuality, grooming, and how you handle a torn sock - mirror your inner values and discipline.

- **Responsibility and integrity:** Owning your actions, even when no one is watching, builds trust and creates a culture of excellence.

- **Habits shape destiny:** Repeated habits, good or bad, quietly determine your trajectory; breaking unhelpful patterns demands patience and determination.

- **Choice is power:** You can complain like a duck or rise like an eagle; attitude is always a choice, and change begins the moment you decide differently.

- **Value people and details:** Recognising the contribution of every person and honouring small details cultivates humility and true greatness.

Reflect & Apply

Use these prompts to put the chapter into practice:

- **Assess your attitude:** Think about your reactions over the past week. Where did a negative attitude colour your response, and what small shift could you make next time?

- **Spot limiting habits:** Identify one recurring behaviour that slows your progress. Choose one new, constructive habit to install in its place.

- **Practise consistency in small things:** Commit to one simple discipline - waking up on time, keeping your workspace tidy, or finishing tasks you start. It reflects a strong attitude.

- **Value the people around you:** Notice and acknowledge someone's effort or contribution today. Observe how this changes your perspective and the relationship.

- **Choose your "bird":** When you face a challenge this week, pause and consciously choose an eagle mindset rather than a duck's complaint. Note how this affects your actions and outcomes.

Every day presents a fresh chance to grow through attitude; when you honour that choice consistently, excellence and success start following you naturally.

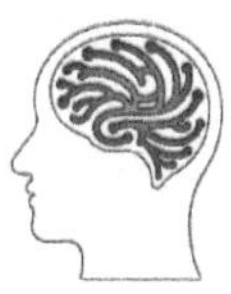

8

Power of Positive Beliefs

~ Believing a solution paves the way to a solution.

Faith Can Move Mountains

One of the most profound and practical truths of success is captured in the timeless phrase: "Faith can move mountains." This isn't just poetic license - it's an invitation to realise the phenomenal power of belief. If you truly believe you can move a mountain, you activate the momentum to do so. Yet, the honest truth remains that many never believe so deeply, and as a result, few ever achieve such feats.

Some sceptics dismiss this notion as fanciful, scoffing, "You can't just tell a mountain to move away and expect it to obey." They mistake genuine belief for wishful thinking. It's true - you can't simply wish away obstacles or magically manifest your dream office, mansion, or leadership role through chants or wishes alone. But belief, when aligned with action and intention, becomes a formidable force that moves metaphorical and literal mountains.

How Belief Transforms Lives

Belief isn't mystical; it's practical psychology and energy combined. The mindset of "I am positive. I can" - generates the drive, capability, and resilience needed to realise goals. It's no accident that most young people entering the workforce silently desire success but falter - because they lack firm belief in their climb. They remain unaware of the steps and commitment required, living within their comfort zone of average.

Conversely, a smaller, determined few adopt a mindset of certainty: "I am going to the top." With unwavering belief, these individuals study and emulate successful leaders - they observe how top achievers think, solve problems, and behave. The knowledge of *how* success occurs naturally flows to those who are convinced it's possible.

Inspiring Tales of Unshakable Belief

Consider the story shared by David J. Schwartz of a young American woman who dared to establish a sales agency for mobile homes. Despite having less than ten thousand US dollars saved, no business experience, and facing stiff competition, she held an unshakable belief in her venture's success. She studied market trends, understood her rivals, and persisted with confidence.

Against the odds, she secured investment, convinced suppliers to provide inventory with no upfront payment, and rapidly scaled her business. What seemed impossible to many became tangible for her, powered by belief.

Belief in the Modern World's Great Endeavours

Belief propels humanity's boldest achievements beyond imagination's limits. Space exploration, once pure fantasy, endures through collective conviction in its possibility, just as the unyielding faith in curing cancer sustains decades of research.

Engineering triumphs like the English Channel Tunnel stand as testaments to this power: first proposed in 1802 and debated in the 1950s, it hinged on leaders' belief it *could* be done. British MP and railway pioneer Sir Edward Watkin championed it passionately in the late 19th century for its economic promise, but realisation came under Prime Ministers Margaret Thatcher and President François Mitterrand - digging began in 1987-88, breakthrough in 1991, and official opening on May 6, 1994. Without that sustained belief, England and Europe might still be divided by more than water.

Closer to home, the remarkable journey of the Ram Mandir exemplifies how sustained belief can reshape history amid controversy and decades of delay. From the 16th century, when Babur's forces razed a Rama temple at his believed birthplace to build the Babri Masjid. The 1992 demolition ignited national shockwaves, the site embodied deep divisions. Post-independence governments, in their partial embrace of secularism long denied Hindus' rightful claim to the site. Yet champions who possessed passionate belief about its existence and socio-economic benefits - like government archaeologist K.K. Muhammed (providing historical evidence), Subramanian Swamy (legal advocacy), VHP leader Ashok Singhal, and scholar Sant Ram Bhadracharya fuelled the movement with unyielding conviction. The 2014-24 government's under by Prime Minister Narendra Modi's, resolve finally led to the 2024 consecration - proof that focused belief, transcending politics and time, turns destiny's obstacles into triumphs.

How Beliefs Grow Within Us?

The Seed Metaphor

The ancient Indian philosophy of Samkhya offers a compelling metaphor: beliefs are seeds planted in the fertile soil of the mind. Like any seed, a belief can grow and bear fruit or wither and fail based on - how it's nurtured.

When we sow positive, empowering beliefs, they flourish into actions and outcomes aligned with growth and fulfilment. When we nurture doubts, fears, and limiting beliefs, the harvest is stagnation and disappointment.

The choice, quite simply, lies in what you choose to believe and how you tend the seeds of your inner garden.

What Produces Failures?

Decades of conversations with those facing business and career setbacks reveal a recurring pattern: doubt and resignation often underpin the collapse. Common confessions include, "I never truly believed it would succeed," "Doubts plagued me from the start," or "Failure was no surprise."

This "I'll try, but it won't work" mindset guarantees defeat - disbelief silently sabotages, crafting excuses to validate itself. Think doubt, invite failure; think victory, attract success.

I once spoke with a struggling fiction writer who admired a celebrated author, saying, "He's brilliant, but I could never reach that level." Her words grieved me, for I knew that writer well - an ordinary mind propelled by extraordinary self-belief.

As David J. Schwartz wisely noted: "Respect leaders, learn from them, but don't worship. Believe you can surpass them. Those who settle for second best get exactly that." Dare to believe big - your thoughts forge your destiny.

The door to opportunity stands wider than ever. Commit today to step through and join those who claim their successes - not by chance, but by design. The path begins with belief. It cannot be ignored.

How to Develop the Power of Belief

Belief is not magic; it is practical, it is real, and it is within your reach. Yoga teaches us that mastery over the mind, the ability to calm its endless fluctuations, is the key to shaping our beliefs. By learning to observe and guide our thoughts and emotions, we can reprogram beliefs that empower instead of limiting us.

Here are three foundational guides to building and strengthening your belief:

1. Think Success, Not Failure:

- Switch your mental programming from "I can't" to "I will."

- When faced with challenges, tell yourself, "I'm going to win," rather than "I might lose."

- In competition, affirm, "I'm on par with the best," instead of "I'm outclassed."

- When opportunity knocks, say, "I can do this," never "I can't."

- Let the dominant thought in your mind be "I will succeed."

- Positive thinking primes your brain to find solutions; negative thinking leads to self-fulfilling failure.

2. Remember Your Worth:

- Success doesn't require genius or luck.

- It's cultivated by ordinary people with extraordinary belief in themselves.

- Don't underestimate your potential or sell yourself short.

3. Believe Big:

- The size of your belief determines the scale of your success.

- Aim high, dream big, and respect the small wins along the way.

- Remember, big ideas and plans are not necessarily more complex than small ones - they often bring greater clarity and momentum.

Exploring Your Beliefs

Beliefs are at the core of your reality - they are the narratives you accept as truth. These narratives don't have to be universal, only true for you. For example: if you believe that the economy during a pandemic won't favour your growth, then that belief creates a limitation. Similarly, beliefs about health, relationships, or personal worth shape what you perceive as possible or impossible.

Self-awareness begins with honesty: What do you believe is lacking in your life? Is it health, financial security, love, or something else? Naming these gaps is the courageous first step toward transformation.

Often, limiting beliefs stem from unconscious acceptance or cultural conditioning, so challenging them is essential. Ask yourself honestly: "Are these beliefs always true? Do they serve me? Which ones hinder my growth?"

The Delete Tool: Reprogram Your Beliefs

To exit limiting patterns, try this simple mental exercise – 'The Delete Tool'. It helps replace negative beliefs with positive, empowering alternatives. Here are some examples:

- Replace "I can't do that" with *"I haven't learned it yet, but I'm willing to grow."*

- Replace "It's lost and I can't find it" with *"It's misplaced; I will find it soon."*

- Replace "They're driving me crazy" with *"They challenge me and help me grow."*

- Replace "My job makes me sick" with *"I will take steps to improve my work or find a better one."*

- Replace "You tickle me to death" with *"You make me laugh endlessly."*

Journaling your current beliefs and consciously reframing them plants the seeds for a fertile mindset, nurturing pathways of resilience, hope, and achievement.

Embracing a New Belief System for Growth and Transformation

Let's open ourselves to a fresh set of beliefs – that nurture growth, healing, and lasting improvement. This new paradigm can truly transform your life:

- Tension and worry are part of life's ebb and flow; peace and calm are our natural resting state.

- Anger may arise as a signal, but compassion is the healing force.

- Hurt is an undeniable experience; empathy connects us through shared humanity.

- True happiness isn't found in possessions or status; it blossoms within each thought and intention.

- Life's challenges may spark competition, yet cooperation is the surest path to harmony.

- Criticism can spur growth, appreciation fuels motivation.

- Love often carries expectations, but unconditional love is about acceptance.

- Guilt can burden the heart; real transformation arises through awareness and understanding.

We naturally strive to improve the quality of our thoughts, yet lasting change requires addressing the root cause: our deeply held beliefs. If your belief system insists that anger is necessary for discipline, or that without strictness things spiral out of control, or that vulnerability means weakness, then you have created barriers to cultivating peace and love.

Consider, instead, adopting beliefs that support tranquillity and kindness. Consider the perspective that individuals, including yourself and others, possess an inherent disposition towards peace and kindness. Such a belief can transform how you navigate adversity, infusing challenges with compassion and grace.

Our subconscious holds many beliefs about ourselves and others. Recognising painful mental scripts is key to changing our inner narrative and finding freedom.

Understanding the Power of Beliefs

Anthony Robbins wisely notes in *Awaken the Giant Within* that our lives aren't defined by what happens to us, but rather by how we understand and respond to those events. The way we interpret our experiences shapes our reality more than the circumstances themselves.

This highlights three core challenges we all face with beliefs:

- Most of our beliefs operate below conscious awareness.

- Many beliefs are founded on misinterpretations of past experiences.

- Once adopted, beliefs are accepted as absolute truth, our personal gospel.

Remarkably, great leaders often defy conventional logic. They craft and hold empowering beliefs about their capabilities and potential that surpass common expectations. Their resilience and success flow from consciously creating motivating mental frameworks.

The turning point for any profound personal breakthrough is when the mind connects intense dissatisfaction with old limiting beliefs alongside the deep satisfaction of new empowering ones.

Practical Exercise: Removing Limiting Beliefs

Take a moment now with pen and paper.

If you're ready to shift your mindset toward positivity and growth, try this simple but powerful exercise, the "delete tool":

- Identify a limiting belief or negative thought you habitually carry.

- Write it down honestly, for example, "I am not good enough."

- Now, consciously replace it with a positive, affirmative statement, for example, "I am capable and constantly growing."

This practice helps sweep away mental clutter, making room for seeds of positive self-belief to take root. Repeated daily, it gradually rewires your subconscious to nurture confidence and proactive thinking.

Integrating Belief & Work with Daily Practice

Take a moment - 5, 10, even 30 seconds - to pause in your day, and reinforce your new positive affirmations. Visualise your success as real and palpable. This mental rehearsal aligns your inner state with your goals and propels you toward fulfilling them.

Remember, true success isn't a one-time event. It's a consistent unfolding of achievements, built step-by-step through deliberate practice and a supportive mindset.

Mindful Meditation for Thought, Attitude and Belief

This meditation practice invites you to vividly picture what you desire - whether it's abundance in money, vibrant health, loving relationships, or personal fulfilment, on an imaginary mental screen before you.

If visualising feels challenging, start by describing these desires in colours, shapes, or sensations. Then, imagine yourself embodying the confidence, posture, and attitude of someone who has already achieved these aspirations. Picture yourself living that joyful, abundant life in the present moment.

At the heart of this practice is cultivating an intense desire to shift your inner attitude - to create ripples that transform your mindset and consequently, your relationships and circumstances. Be honest with yourself: What patterns or attitudes are holding you back? Reflect deeply and acknowledge them.

Feel what it means to succeed - versus feelings of helplessness or doubt:

- Am I capable of this?

- Am I smart enough?

- Can I make this happen?

The answer is a resounding Yes, you can!

Whenever self-doubt creeps in, especially during challenging moments - pause and anchor your attention by pressing your three fingers together for five seconds. As you do, mentally repeat your chosen affirmation or goal. This simple gesture grounds you, just as it does for top athletes, doctors, teachers, and business leaders. Why not for you? You are unique and capable.

To transform your mindset, consistency is key. Practice this daily and align your actions with your intentions.

See Appendix 4 – Affirmations and Manifestations

Guided Meditation - For Thoughts, Attitudes and Beliefs

It's Time to Take Charge

Buddhism's Middle Path promotes balance, steering clear of both extreme optimism and pessimism to encourage a practical approach to life.

Your daily experiences serve as a free laboratory for self-discovery - observe, experiment, and learn from every interaction and situation to foster growth.

Daily affirmations serve as a powerful foundation for building confidence and success-oriented thinking. But to truly unlock your subconscious potential and manifest your deepest dreams, you need to go further.

Harness the Law of Attraction by raising your energetic frequency - align your thoughts, emotions, and actions so that the right people, opportunities, and resources are naturally drawn to you. Living in harmony with the universe's vibrations cultivates deeper happiness, peace, and abundance.

Discover the secret to intentionally creating and receiving the life you desire. You are not a passive bystander but an active co-creator of your reality, equipped with ancient wisdom and modern tools.

Chapter Summary

This chapter demonstrates how **belief** can profoundly influence the course of your life. Genuine faith, not vague hoping - provides the energy, courage, and focus needed to face obstacles and steer your path with confidence. Belief is not magic; it is the practical mindset of **"I am positive, I can"** that turns ordinary individuals into extraordinary achievers.

Key ideas to carry forward are:

- **Belief as a catalyst:** Successful change always begins with a deep belief in your own potential and in the possibility of success.

- **Beliefs shape reality:** Positive, empowering beliefs promote growth and bold action, while limiting beliefs quietly slow or sabotage your progress.

- **Challenge and delete:** Questioning your assumptions and using tools like the mental **"delete tool"** can interrupt negative patterns and replace them with supportive ones.

- **See the hidden scripts:** Regular self-reflection reveals the often-unseen beliefs driving your behaviour and results.

- **Balanced belief:** Neither blind optimism nor chronic pessimism is helpful; a grounded, hopeful mindset supports steady progress and inner peace.

- **Law of Attraction link:** Harnessing the Law of Attraction means aligning your thoughts, feelings, and energy with the opportunities you wish to attract.

- **Practices that reinforce belief:** Consistent meditation and affirmations strengthen empowering beliefs and align your daily actions with your goals.

Reflect & Apply

Use these prompts to put the chapter into practice:

- **Reflect:** Identify 2–3 beliefs that may be limiting your success. What recurring negative thoughts or assumptions keep showing up? Write them down.

- **Apply the delete tool:** Each day, consciously replace one limiting belief with a specific, positive affirmation - such as "I am capable," "I am learning fast," or "I am progressing every day."

- **Integrate meditation:** During mindfulness or quiet time, repeat your affirmations and visualise yourself already living the success you seek. Feel the confidence and calm in your body.

- **Grow your environment:** Seek new perspectives, books, mentors, and associations that challenge your old stories and reinforce your new, empowering beliefs.

- **Commit to the process:** Remember that lasting success is built over time. Stay persistent and patient, feeding your mind with positive thoughts, steady action, and an open heart.

By cultivating a balanced, resilient mind through regular practice, you root your growth in reality while opening yourself to universal laws - like the Law of Attraction, that amplify your journey toward lasting abundance.

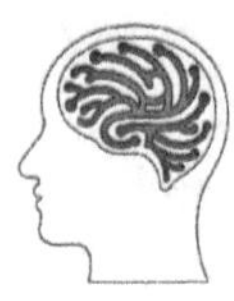

9

Power of Sensory Faculties

~ Using Visual, Auditory, and Kinaesthetic Senses to Transform Your Life.

The Power of Perception

Life, as it turns out, comes equipped with a control panel - our senses. Imagine if, at any moment, it were possible to boost the volume on joy, dim the lights on pain, or remix memories as if editing a home movie. The power lies in how we use our five faculties - sight, sound, touch, taste, and smell. But most of our experience is sculpted by the top three: Visual, Auditory, and Kinaesthetic (VAK).

The strength of each sense means a huge difference in human perception. They are also referred to as VAK (Visual-Auditory-Kinaesthetic). Two people can see the same traffic accident but offer utterly different accounts. One may have paid more attention to what he saw and another to what he heard. These perceptions become internal filters through which future experiences are interpreted.

Senses Shape Reality

During my Navy days as Squadron Commander of Missile Boats and Commanding Officer of INS Pralay in Vizag, I dealt with a tricky harbour entry. Two Lieutenants, Jaspreet Shergill and Manoj Kumar, reported on the same fog patch: Shergill described seeing a dense cloud near the tanker jetty while Manoj Kumar noted a faint rumble masking engine sounds. Both observed the same situation from different perspectives.

Reflections

This was my lightbulb moment - it was not just psychology, but operational safety. Leadership meant learning who responded to what cues: one thrived on images, another on sounds. And this key insight, knowing your sensory code, became their compass amid uncertainty.

People perceive accidents differently, each forming unique mental impressions based on what they focus on. These sensory filters shape our future actions and emotions. Change involves two steps: shifting how we feel by altering our physical state and updating our behaviour by modifying internal images.

With practice, this process becomes a form of mental engineering. Some achieve their goals through vivid visualisation, others prefer a gentle approach, and for some, a tactile cue like squeezing a stress ball boosts motivation.

The Sub-Modality Toolkit

Discovering which sensory "knobs" move us - brightness, tone, softness, intensity, puts power back in our hands. Once we learn what works, we're no longer at the mercy of old habits or memories. Instead, we become artists and engineers of our inner world:

- Visual thinkers light up with bright, high-definition images.

- Auditory minds need just the right volume and timbre.

- Kinaesthetic folks come alive through texture, temperature, and emotional resonance.

By consciously choosing and experimenting with these inputs, we rewire how we see challenges, rehearse victories, and recover from setbacks.

Don't underestimate the power of a well-chosen filter. Leaders, coaches, and parents who master this become beacons for others, even when "success" looks improbable from the outside.

Associated or Disassociated

A powerful tip: how you frame your mental "movie" matters.

- **Associated:** Reliving the scene as a participant, feeling every heartbeat.

- **Disassociated:** Observing yourself from the outside, like an audience member.

Both have their uses. One immerses, the other protects. Learning to switch frames is the hallmark of emotional mastery and a secret weapon in your inner toolbox.

List of Terms for Possible Sub-Modalities

Visual

• Movie or still frames	• Intensity of colour (or B&W)
• Panorama or framed (shape)	• Degree of contrast
• Colour or B&W	• Movement – fast, slow, or stationary
• Brightness	• Focus – which parts are in or out.
• Size of picture (large, small)	• Intermittent or steady focus
• Size of central objects	• Angle viewed from
• Self in or out of the picture	• Number of pictures
• Distance of picture from self	• Location
• 3-D quality	• Others?
• 3-D quality	

Auditory

• Volume	• Tonality
• Cadence (interruptions, groupings)	• Timbre (quality, resonating form)
• Rhythm (regular, irregular)	• Uniqueness of sound (gravely, smooth)
• Inflexions (words marked out, how)	• Sound moves around – spatial
• Tempo	• Location – far / near
• Pause	• Others?

Kinaesthetic

• Temperature	• Steady – intermittent
• Texture	• Intensity
• Vibration	• Weight
• Pressure	• Density
• Movement	• Location
• Duration	• Others?

For Pain/Sensation

• Tingling	• Duration
• Hot – cold	• Intermittent (such as throbbing)
• Muscle tension	
• Sharp – dull	• Location
• Pressure	• Others?

Activity – Meditation Exercise for VAK – Positive / Pleasant Images

Notice what happens to your feelings now. People respond differently, especially to kinaesthetic cues. Many find that making an image brighter or larger intensifies it, placing you in a more positive, resourceful state.

Observe someone's mind through their physiology. Breathing deepens, shoulders straighten, face relaxes, and the whole body becomes more alert. Now, let's try the same exercise with negative images.

See Appendix 2: VAK Sensory Meditation

Guided Meditation – Positive and Pleasant Images

Activity – Meditation Exercise for VAK – Negative / Unpleasant Images

What happens to your negative image during this process? Most find the image loses power – it becomes less painful or even disappears. You can take a painful memory and watch it dissolve.

You can live in one of two ways: letting your mind run its habitual course or consciously running it. By implanting cues you choose, you create more energy, joy, and passion in life.

"There is nothing good or bad but thinking maketh it so."

– William Shakespeare

See Appendix 2: VAK Sensory Meditation

Guided Meditation – Negative and unpleasant Images

The Power of Language

Language shapes our internal representations:

- What do you mean when you say someone has a *bright future?*

- How do you feel when someone says the *future looks dim?*

- What does it mean when you say you're *dropping your child to school?*

- How do you interpret phrases like *weighs heavily on the mind* or *mental block?*

- What about *blew it out of proportion?*

These aren't mere metaphors. Often, they precisely describe our inner experience. Recall when you enlarged an unpleasant memory – how did that affect your state? Such words directly influence our behaviour.

When you catch yourself revisiting old arguments in your head, lower the intensity of your inner voice. If limiting thoughts arise, change their tone - make them playful or flirtatious and notice if this shifts your motivation.

Activity

Relax and form a clear mental picture of what motivates you. Pause and ask yourself:

- Do you see a movie or a snapshot?

- Is it in colour or black & white?

- Is it close or far?

- Is it left, right, or centre?

- Is it high, low, or in the middle of your vision?

- Is it associated – through your own eyes?

- Is it disassociated – like watching yourself from outside?

- Does it have a frame, or is it a panorama?

- Is it bright or dim? Dark or light?

- Is it focused or unfocused?

As you answer, notice which sub modalities have the greatest intensity for you. Now, do the same for your auditory and kinaesthetic senses:

- Do you hear your own voice or others?

- Is it dialogue or monologue?

- Are sounds loud or quiet?

- Is the tempo slow or fast?

- Are sounds steady or intermittent?

- What is the main thing you hear or say?

- Where is the sound located?

- When you feel it, is it hard or soft? Warm or cool?

- Rough or smooth? Flexible or rigid?

- Solid or liquid? Sour or sweet?

- Where is the feeling located in your body?

Some questions may be challenging at first. Those with kinaesthetic-dominant representation may find visualising tough; auditory dominants may first hear sounds; kinaesthetic individuals may struggle with visuals or sounds. As you practice, you'll learn which sub-modalities powerfully affect your mental states.

As a Modeller

Always be curious about how someone produces a result, mental or physical.

- For example, when someone says, *"I am so depressed,"* I don't ask *why* - that only deepens the state. Instead, I ask *how* they do it.

- Questions like: *What do you picture? What are you saying to yourself? How do you say it? What tone do you use?* These mental and physical actions create specific emotional results.

- Change the structure of these processes, and the state shifts away from depression.

- Suppose someone loves their work, but you don't and you want to. Learn what creates that feeling for them. You'll be amazed at how quickly you can change.

- Remember, frustration, depression, and ecstasy aren't fixed things. They're processes created by mental images, sounds, and physical actions that we consciously or unconsciously control.

- Like any skill, this takes repetition and practice. The more often you cue these simple sub-modality shifts, the faster you can produce the results you want.

These changes are significant, but how do you lock them in? Through a process I call the **Whoosh Pattern**, which, once mastered, happens automatically, without conscious effort.

Whoosh Pattern – Process

- **Step 1:** Identify the behaviour you wish to change. For example, if you want to stop biting your fingernails, visualise yourself about to bite them.

- **Step 2:** Create a new mental picture of the desired behaviour. Imagine refraining from biting, applying gentle pressure to the finger you would bite, and seeing your nails perfectly manicured. This new image should be disassociated, as if you are watching it from the outside.

- **Step 3:** Now, "whoosh" the two images together so that the unhelpful, old picture automatically triggers the new, resourceful one, leading to positive change in your behaviour.

The key to this technique is speed and most importantly, having fun. You tell your mind: see this, whoosh, do this; see this, whoosh, do this; see this... whoosh until the old habit automatically cues the new, desired behaviour. For best results, practice in sub conscious state – mindful meditation.

See Appendix 2: VAK Sensory Meditation

Guided Meditation – Whoosh Pattern

Don't Find Fault, Find A Remedy

How Your Mind Can Sabotage Love and Well-being

Depression is not a fixed life sentence like a lost limb; it is a shifting mental state people move into and out of. When feeling low, many quietly push their happy memories far away - small, faded, and distant. While the painful experiences are recalled big, close, and emotionally intense. This distorted inner "editing" makes life look darker than it really is, and ruins not just mood but also how we relate to others.

The same mechanism operates in relationships. In the beginning, love feels magical because the mind zooms in on the intoxicating qualities of the other person and gently blurs their flaws. Over time, the focus often reverses. Instead of reliving the warmth of that first walk, first kiss, or first shared joke, the mind replays small irritations - the toothpaste cap, the forgotten message, last night's harsh word and makes these moments big and vivid. Mid-argument, simply choosing to recall and "bring closer" a tender memory can soften anger and reconnect you to why you chose each other in the first place.

Henry Ford's advice, "Don't find fault, find a remedy," applies perfectly here. Modern psychology and even quantum physics suggest that change does not always require long, slow struggle; systems often "jump" from one state to another in an instant. In the same way, when you consciously change how you picture, hear, and feel your experiences, the sub-modalities of your inner movie - you can create surprisingly rapid shifts in mood, love, and connection.

Process to Alleviate Pain

The mind creates pain only when it receives sensory input signalling pain. Then do this activity:

- Describe your pain's sub-modalities.

- Some pain felt heavy, others light; some large and bright, others small.

- Change these sub-modalities: disassociate from the pain and see it outside yourself.

- Visualise the pain's shape and size, place it ten feet away.

- Make the image of pain grow and explode, then shrink.

- Now, imagine pushing the pain into the sun, watching it melt away, and descending as sunshine nourishing plants.

- After this, 90% reported their headaches diminished within five minutes.

A Transformative Tale from a Training Room

Not long ago, during a corporate training session in Mumbai, I noticed a subtle but telling pattern. Nearly every attendee was carrying a heavy load - not just metaphorically, but quite visibly. Faces etched with tension, furrowed brows, and in hushed whispers, complaints of persistent headaches. The space was far from inviting - stifling with poor airflow, and harsh, unforgiving lighting that seemed to amplify discomfort rather than soothe it.

What became clear to me was this profound truth: the mind only creates pain when it receives sensory signals that translate as pain. Essentially, pain is not fixed; it's a process, a conversation between body, mind, and senses.

I invited the group to pinpoint the qualities of their own pain - to explore its texture, size, brightness, volume. Participants shared: for some, the pain was a dense, throbbing presence. For others, a faint flicker, distant and muted. Some held images of vast, fiery pools of discomfort; others saw tiny shadows, quiet yet nagging.

Then came the magic. I guided them through a simple but powerful practice:

First, disassociate, step outside the pain. Visualise it as an object, safely placed at a distance - say, ten paces away.

Then, imagine that image swelling, growing so large it bursts through the ceiling, spilling light where once there was darkness. Suddenly, let it shrink down, becoming smaller and smaller until it almost vanishes.

Finally, with a playful twist, envision pushing that pain toward the blazing sun, watching as it melts away into golden rays that drift softly to earth, showering warmth and nourishment over tender plants.

The result? Almost instantly, the room stirred with surprise and delight - over 90% of participants reported their headaches fading, some even disappearing altogether, all within minutes.

Isn't this a phenomenon we've all glimpsed? That moment when pain retreats, distracted by life's marvels or a good laugh? It's the power of changing how we represent our experience, choosing to edit the mental film rather than be edited by it.

With these tools, we hold the key to transforming not only our pain, but our lives and to brightening the lives of those around us. The journey to mastery lies in a simple choice: to become directors of our own inner cinema, navigating the script, the soundtrack, and the scenes with conscious intention.

How Will This Organise Your Life?

You will learn to organise your life. How?

- Start your day right: A rushed, stressed morning usually sets the tone for the entire day.

- Prioritise your goals: Designing clear goals helps reset your mind for success in career, relationships, and health.

- Define balance for yourself: What does balance mean to you?

- Say 'yes', by learning to say 'no': Avoid being a people-pleaser who neglects their own needs.

- Schedule time out: Regular breaks are essential to reset.

- Set and maintain boundaries: Early boundary-setting accelerates positive change.

- Disconnect to reconnect: Switch off devices to listen to your inner self.

- Let it go: Release overwhelming to-do lists, control issues, others' expectations, judgments, and excuses like "I don't have time."

Cut through excuses that block your balance and edge you closer to burnout. Be your own VIP. Self-care is not selfish - if you don't prioritise yourself, who will?

When Change May Not Happen (Yet)

While many readers experience genuine shifts through mindfulness and belief work, not everyone will fully reverse depression, restlessness, or other inner struggles. Some live with deep clinical conditions, long-standing trauma, strong biological factors, or life situations that constantly re-trigger pain. In such cases, the tools in this book are supportive but not sufficient alone; they need to be combined with medical care, therapy, or specialised help. Change also demands personal readiness, responsibility, and regular practice - reading without doing, or hoping without acting, naturally limits results.

The Crucial Role of Family and Environment

Inner transformation does not happen in a vacuum. A supportive spouse, children, and close family can act like emotional oxygen - using kind language, encouraging small practices, and refusing to label the person as "hopeless" or "always like this." Their steady patience and respect can dramatically speed up recovery. By contrast, constant criticism, mockery, or casual negativity from relatives, neighbours, or friends can quietly undo weeks of inner work, reinforcing the old identity. Learning to gently set boundaries - reducing time with negative influences, not absorbing hurtful comments, and consciously seeking uplifting company, is part of mental hygiene. Your inner kitchen needs clean ingredients: your own effort, loving family support, and wise distance from those who repeatedly pollute your mind-space.

Chapter Summary

This chapter reveals the profound power of your **sensory faculties** as the control panel through which you experience and shape reality. Each person's inner world is uniquely organised around a dominant sensory style - **Visual, Auditory, or Kinaesthetic (VAK)** and learning your pattern helps you understand why you respond the way you do.

Key ideas to carry forward are:

- **Senses shape reality:** Your dominant modality colours how you remember events, make decisions, and react under pressure.

- **Edit your inner "film":** Recognising your sensory preferences enables you to consciously adjust your internal movie - its brightness, volume, distance, and intensity, so you can change your mood and behaviour.

- **The "Whoosh Pattern":** This technique blends old, unhelpful mental images with new, empowering ones, enabling rapid shifts in habits and emotional responses.

- **Language as a lever:** Words do not just describe experience; they actively influence it. The phrases you use about yourself and your life can either reinforce pain or unlock new possibilities.

- **Sub-modality shifts:** Practising small tweaks in visual, auditory, and kinaesthetic sub-modalities teaches you how to change state on demand and reprogram limiting patterns.

- Associated vs. disassociated frames: Stepping *into* a memory (associated) helps you feel and learn from it deeply, while stepping *out* (disassociated) lets you observe and heal with objectivity.

- **Self-care and connection:** Setting boundaries, making time to relax, and letting go help maintain emotional well-being, while support from loved ones is vital for personal growth.

Reflect & Apply

Use these prompts to move from awareness to practical skill:

- **Reflect:** Recall a recent moment of emotional or physical discomfort. Which senses dominated—images, sounds, or sensations? Was your inner "film" bright, loud, close, or dim and distant? How might changing these settings alter your response?

- **Apply:** During your next stressful or painful experience, practise disassociating: see the scene from a distance, shrink or fade it, then replace it using the **Whoosh Pattern** with a calmer, more resourceful image. Notice how your state shifts.

- **Engage:** Listen to your daily self-talk. What words and metaphors do you habitually use? Begin consciously choosing more empowering language to recode your inner script.

- **Extend:** Identify your dominant VAK style. Then, tailor your learning, communication, and motivation - more visuals, richer sound, or stronger physical cues, to match it in work and relationships.

- **Integrate:** Create daily habits that honour your senses: limit digital overload, set clear boundaries, and prioritise rest and quiet so your sensory system can reset and support mindful, intentional living.

This chapter highlights that while events may be the same, perception is personal and by mastering your sensory codes, you reclaim the power to rewrite your experience. *(Adapted from Tony Robbins' seminar "Unleash the Power Within", 1999.)*

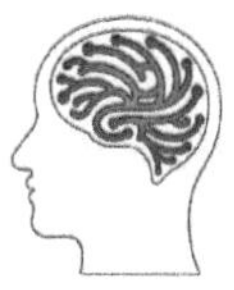

1 0

Power of Purpose

*~ Nothing can stop you from achieving your goals
when you know your purpose.*

Finding True Direction Through Purpose

Without a clear purpose, it is difficult to have a clear direction in life. When setting goals, it is crucial to understand that they should not be imposed by external sources. Instead, they must arise from your inner motivations. Remember, people lose their way when they lose sight of their why.

Many attempt lifestyle design by modelling themselves after someone else. However, this approach is mistaken. Lifestyle design is about accepting who you are and aligning your needs with your purpose, not copying an online guru or lifestyle design 'expert'. The more you learn about yourself, the better equipped you will be to create a unique lifestyle that resonates with your values, needs, abilities and motivations, making you feel more connected to your true self.

There are countless reasons why people seek to transform their lives. You might be motivated to get out of debt, become financially independent, gain more control over your life, spend more time with family, travel more, focus on your passion or reduce stress.

Regardless of your motivation, transformation begins by making your work, work for you. You must first understand yourself to learn how you want to work. It is the most important subject you will ever know, and the key to your personal growth and inspiration - inspiring you to take the necessary steps towards life transformation. Let me share a story from my life.

Do You Have a Clear Vison?

Over 20 years ago, while teaching a class in Mumbai at Wigan and Leigh College of Management, I instructed students on accessing their minds to programme any abilities they desired in life. A young woman approached me and asked, 'Can you teach me how to be a faster typist?' I asked her what she meant. Why did she want to be faster? She replied, 'Because I work in data entry and the more data I enter, the more I get paid.'

If you have unlocked the powers of your mind, perhaps you want something bigger. So, I asked, 'You want to be a faster typist to earn more. But why do you want to earn more?' She said, 'I want to grow my savings.'

I said, 'Good, we're getting somewhere. Why do you want to grow savings?' She answered, 'Because I am trying to buy a home.' I said, 'Good. That's even better. Why do you want to buy a home?'

She explained, 'My mother lives in Delhi, which is unsafe. I want her to move to Mumbai and live with me in my house.' Now we were getting closer. 'Why do you want your mother to live with you?'

'Well,' she said, 'we are the last two surviving family members. In my mother's home in Delhi, we have many family heirlooms and antiques. I want to move it all to Mumbai and decorate our family legacy so that my children will never forget their heritage.'

I replied, 'Amazing. That's what you're really after. Now, why focus only on being a faster typist?'

Reflections

Each one of us comes into this life with a unique purpose. We are here to be, do, or create something particular that enhances those around us and brings us the greatest joy and deepest fulfilment.

The first step to living that life is to DECODE your life's purpose. DECODE will help you do this. The next natural step is to create a clear vision aligned with your true calling, giving you something inspiring to live into. You will learn to design purpose-driven goals that blend scientific insight with spiritual wisdom.

Are My Goals Programmed into Me?

Our goals are often programmed into us through society's setup, advertising, the media, and politicians who shape how we think. Very frequently, the goals we chase are simply those that have been programmed into us. These are not truly our own desires but rather the desires of others that we are led to believe in and the goals that enrich businesses or fulfil societal expectations. This is why many people wake up one day in their forties wondering what happened to their life.

As Andrew Carnegie put it, *"If you want to be happy, set a goal that commands your thoughts, liberates your energy, and inspires your hopes."*

I want to share three important questions, a framework that will help you unplug from society's versions of what you should want. This framework will guide you to listen deeply to your innermost self and identify what your soul truly desires.

I have come to believe that we are not merely human beings; we are beings having a human experience. Each soul chooses this life and this human body to experience something unique in this lifetime.

So, wherever you find yourself – whether stuck at home feeling anxious, annoyed and depressed about the coronavirus situation, wildly successful, or struggling, you may feel there is something more out there for you, even if there is a lot of confusion.

Your soul has chosen your current situation as a challenge for learning and growth. It does not wish to set goals that force you off your true path.

Now, let us explore the three most important questions. These form a framework designed to help you understand the difference between goals that arise from within and goals imposed from outside. The framework centres on Experience, Growth, and Contribution, and it can guide you to set meaningful and fulfilling goals. I will explain these in more detail shortly, but first, let us understand the different types of goals.

Types Of Goals: Means Goals and End Goals

It is important to distinguish between means goals and end goals. Means goals are the steps we take to achieve our end goals. They are the smaller, more immediate objectives that lead us to our ultimate aims. End goals, on the other hand, are the final objectives we strive towards. Recognising this difference helps us set more purposeful and fulfilling goals in life.

A means goal is a means to an end, while an end goal is the ultimate destination. For instance, the goal might be to get good grades so you can attend a good university, complete a law degree, become a lawyer, then work hard at university to achieve good marks again, secure a job and grow professionally, so that eventually you own a home, take holidays, and retire comfortably. All these steps in between are means to an end.

But what is the true end that people are chasing? Many do not know their true end goal. What was the outcome in the story I shared at the beginning?

She did not understand the difference between end and means goals. Being a faster typist was a means to an end, not the purpose itself. Therefore, she was unable to set her goals effectively because her purpose was unclear. What do you want to aim for - the end or the means?

Finding your purpose and designing your end goals happens in the subconscious mind.

Why the subconscious mind? Because we must give our subconscious mind the end goal and then be open to allow it to guide us to the right opportunities, paths, and actions that will lead us there.

If you focus on being a faster typist, you will lose momentum and energy if you lack passion. She did not have a passion for typing faster but rather for having a home where she could imagine her future children running around and decorating it with family heirlooms. Being a faster typist was not the fastest way to reach that dream.

There may be a better and quicker way. She may not know it now, but her subconscious will figure it out. Designing goals subconsciously, at the Alpha level, when you have better self-awareness - comes through meditation and deep reflection.

Having explored the difference between means goals and end goals, and seen why your energy must ultimately serve the latter, a natural question arises: how will you actually *design* your goals so they stay true to your deeper purpose?

Beyond Vision Boards

In many workshops and corporate trainings, people are invited to create "vision boards": dream posters covered with images, words, and affirmations that represent the life they want - health, relationships, income, lifestyle. Brian Tracy, for instance, teaches vision boards as one visual tool within a larger system of clear goals, written plans, visualisation, and daily action to keep your future emotionally vivid. Used well, such boards can support motivation, but they often start from the outside in, borrowing other people's definitions of success.

In this book, the sequence is reversed: first uncover your inner "why", then design your "what". Purpose work goes deeper than a collage of attractive pictures; it helps you distinguish means from end goals and anchors your choices in the Experiences, Growth, and Contribution that truly matter to you. When purpose is clear, every goal becomes a servant of your "why," not a random image on a wall. It becomes a mirror of your soul's own direction.

Goal Designing

With this foundation, you are now in a stronger position to decide which goals deserve your time and life energy. You are invited to aim for End Goals, not just Means Goals, recognising that the latter are steps or activities that lead to something else rather than being the true destination of your journey.

What Exactly Is an End Goal?

Consider these examples:

- The need to feel like a father or mother, holding a newborn baby in your arms - a truly beautiful end goal.

- Waking up beside the person you love - that too is a meaningful end goal.

- Owning a home, you can decorate and call your own is also a wonderful end goal.

What Is a Means Goal?

Means goals usually carry materialistic emotions. If your goals are framed as, "I need to get this to get that," they are likely means goals. They often reflect societal norms, which I refer to as "bum norms." These norms stem from societal programming and are not always true or necessary. For example, a common "bum norm" in India once prescribed that true success meant having two SUVs, a farmhouse, and two children. That was the Indian dream in 2000, but it no longer holds the same weight today. Why pursue such goals if they no longer resonate? They are merely bum norms.

To clarify your thinking, here is a simple checklist to distinguish between means and end goals. Take pen and paper and write down your goals. Then ask yourself: is this a means or an end?

How do you know you are pursuing an end goal? End goals are guided by your intellect and passion; there is something about them that genuinely appeals to you. Secondly, end goals are about feelings rather than possessions. Remember the earlier examples: the feeling of holding your newborn child, waking up next to your loved one - it's about the emotions and connection rather than the material surroundings. If your room looks beautiful, would you care about the brand of the sheets, or the family background of your partner? It's about the feeling you experience.

Good advertising often programmes objects into our desires, but your feelings are the true measure of your happiness. Thus, end goals ultimately direct you towards feelings, not material things. How do you ensure you pursue end goals when setting goals? Let me share a story which might resonate with you.

Meaningless Goals

A farmer had a dog that used to sit by the roadside, waiting for vehicles. Whenever a vehicle approached, the dog would chase it, barking loudly. One day, a neighbour asked the farmer, "Do you think your dog will ever catch a car?" The farmer replied, "That is not what bothers me. What worries me is what he would do if he ever caught one."

Reflections

This story serves as a powerful analogy for our pursuit of goals. Often, we chase things without understanding their true significance or what we would do if we achieved them. Many people behave like that dog, pursuing meaningless goals. Mindful meditation can help you uncover your purpose in life by increasing self-awareness. Your purpose consists of the core motivating aims - the reasons you get up each morning.

Your purpose is not merely a guiding light, but a transformative force. It shapes your decisions and infuses your life with meaning and direction. For some, it is found in their vocation - work that fulfils and satisfies beyond just earning a living.

Unlock Your Purpose

This is where the three important questions come in. These questions are part of an exercise that you will undertake. They will help you gain a clear vision of your end goals, quickly and effectively. And here's the trick:

- What experiences or feelings do I want?

- How will I contribute to the world?

- How do I need to grow?

What Experiences or Feelings Do I Want?

We will work through these questions in sequence, beginning with experiences, moving to contribution and finally growth. This exercise will clarify your vision and connect your goals with your deepest purpose. Following are some examples of experiences:

- An example of experience might be travelling to seven countries by train with a camera and photographing all the beautiful things.

- Another example might be being able to coach and share what I have learned.

- Another example of experience might be dining in a particular restaurant in London that you have read about.

- Yet another example of experience might be being able to rent a motorcycle and ride across South America.

- Yet another example could be being the best Indian engineer to design an eco-friendly Setu Samudram (sea bridge) in Palk Strait.

When Personal Dreams Serve a Larger Purpose

The second question focuses on contribution. Having had these experiences and grown as a person, how will you give back to the world? Here, you reflect on service and what actions you might take for the benefit of humanity. Ask yourself: how will my experiences and growth help others? What steps must I take to make a positive impact? Take above examples:

- **Travelling to seven countries by train with a camera.** This experience can become contribution if you use your photographs and stories to inspire others - through talks, books, exhibitions, or social media. You can appreciate culture, history, environment, or simple living, and perhaps support local artisans or causes you encounter on the way. Your joy becomes education and encouragement for others.

- **Dining in a special restaurant in London.** On the surface it is a private pleasure. But you can turn it into learning: studying service, leadership, systems, and team culture - then bringing those insights back into your training, writing, or mentoring. Your luxurious meal becomes a case study that improves how others design experiences for their own customers and teams.

- **Riding a motorcycle across South America.** This can feed your courage, resilience, and cross-cultural understanding. Those qualities then flow into your coaching, helping clients face their own fears and step into the unknown. You might also choose to raise funds or awareness for a cause during such a ride, turning the adventure into a moving campaign.

- **Owning a grand farmhouse.** A farmhouse can be more than a private retreat. It can host retreats for youth, caregivers, veterans, or changemakers at subsidised rates; become a space for organic farming and local employment; or serve as a quiet sanctuary where you create books and courses that touch thousands. The property becomes infrastructure for service, not just status.

- **Designing an ecofriendly Setu Samudram bridge.** Here the contribution is direct: engineering excellence that respects nature, improves trade and travel, and creates livelihoods. The inner intention, to solve problems with minimal harm, makes the "experience" a gift to future generations.

Turning Experiences into Contribution

Even the most personal-sounding experiences - travel, dining, adventure, or a dream home, can be aligned with contribution when you ask, "How will this help me grow, and how will that growth flow back to others?" In this way, your joy and the world's benefit stop being opposites and become partners in your purpose.

Tata Group, for instance, runs large, profitable companies while also investing heavily in rural skill development, education, and healthcare through initiatives like Tata Strive and Tata Trusts, impacting thousands of young people across India.

A successful trainer or corporate executive can follow a similar arc by choosing a clear, service-based purpose - such as using communication and leadership skills to uplift under-resourced youth and then designing career decisions around it, from pro-bono workshops in government schools to funding scholarships and mental-health support. Over time, their brand rests not only on professional success but also on visible social upliftment, turning every keynote, book, and rupee saved into a quiet, continuous contribution to a more skilled and hopeful world.

Your desires first form thoughts and ideas, then words before leading to actions. Understanding the link between desire and action is key.

How Do I Grow?

The third question to ask yourself is: how do I grow to become the person who can experience all that I desire? Growth involves not just acquiring new skills but also evolving personally - physically, mentally, and emotionally. For example:

- If you want to backpack across South America, learning Spanish might be essential.

- Dreaming of global travel? Consider a course in photography to capture your experiences.

- Starting a software company? You'll likely need to master computer applications.

- Aspiring to become an author? Writing classes can sharpen your craft.

- To excel as an Indian chef, learning from culinary scriptures and apprenticeships is invaluable.

- Achieving engineering excellence requires focused study in your chosen discipline.

- Running your first marathon demands disciplined training and fitness routines.

Take time to list how you want to grow. Reflect on the three interconnected questions: What experiences am I seeking? What do I contribute? And soon, we'll explore - How do I grow?

Your personal growth journey is your most powerful tool in realising your goals. It not only unlocks your potential but also equips you to make meaningful contributions and take control of your destiny.

Understanding how you must grow is crucial, but growth must translate into action. The nature of your actions, their intention and focus - determines the impact you have on yourself and the world around you.

Let's now explore the different types of actions and how the quality of your intentions shapes your path.

What Are Different Types of Actions?

Janki Santoke, a Vedanta teacher and senior disciple of Swami Parthasarathy, describes human actions in three broad categories:

- **Selfish Actions:** These benefit your own body, mind, and emotions. They focus on personal care and self-growth.

- **Unselfish Actions:** These are aimed at helping others - family, community, or country and caring for their wellbeing and growth.

- **Selfless Actions:** These occur without expectation of benefit for anyone's body, mind, or emotions but serve a higher purpose, like humanity or the universe.

To illustrate the importance of intention, consider this tale from Ayodhya in India, during the construction of the Shri Ram Temple.

A passerby asked three stone cutters what they were doing.

The first said, "I'm working just to survive."

The second replied, "I'm working to provide for my family's survival."

The third proudly said, "I'm building a temple so thousands can worship here, making Ayodhya a place of pilgrimage and employment."

Though all three performed the same physical task, their intentions differed profoundly. This teaches us that it's not just what we do, it's the attitude and purpose behind our actions that truly matters.

Discovering and Defining Your Life Purpose

How Do You Find Your Purpose?

When you combine the three elements we discussed - Experiences, Contribution, and Growth you will see how they connect in a meaningful way. If you put them down on paper, your sheet might look like this:

EXPERIENCES	CONTRIBUTION	GROWTH
1.		
2.		
3.		

You can write your thoughts under each heading. We are going to take you through this exercise now, but before you start, let me share why this works.

A shipping manager from Dubai, Captain Rohan, attended one of my workshops and wrote down this purpose: *"I want to inspire people to follow their dreams, have a healthy mind and strong body, speak at TEDx, and have a super-efficient mind."*

After listing his three most important purposes, remarkable things began to happen. Clarity emerged in his life, and coincidences and synchronicities started aligning with his goals. For example, he participated in the Dubai Biker Challenge race, came first, and won a prize of one million dollars. The rest is history. Now, let's do this for you.

Sample Purpose Statement

Finally, combine the above questions into one clear statement: the qualities you enjoy expressing, how you express them, the skills you need to develop, and your vision for an ideal world. When crafted carefully, this purpose statement will clarify your direction, inspire meaningful action, and give you confidence and control on your journey.

"Inspiring and empowering people through education and mindfulness, to live their highest vision in a context of love and joy in harmony, with the highest good of all concerned."

Do you see how this statement blends the three key elements?

This has been my life's purpose for many years and has motivated me to transform hundreds of lives through books, workshops, and programmes.

What's Your Purpose?

The secret to living a life filled with joy, meaning, and abundance is to discover your purpose and then use it like a compass to guide you towards your passions and dreams.

Your purpose is what fuels your motivation when things get tough. It answers that recurring question: *"Why the heck am I doing this again?"*

When you know your purpose, nothing can stop you from achieving your goals. Even when obstacles arise, you will find the inner strength and willpower to overcome them and keep moving towards your dreams.

Swami A Parthasarathy, the renowned Vedantic philosopher, writes in his book *Governing Business and Relationships*: *"It's important to know that your purpose changes and evolves and can even change from year to year. As you change and gain more experience and perspective, you will discover new insights into your greatest gifts and how you want to express them in the world."*

For this reason, it's wise to revisit and refine your purpose annually to ensure it still fits your life or needs evolving.

How Do You Discover Your Purpose?

One day, a student asked me, *"The Bhagavad Gita says to shed desires. If I shed desires, how can I have goals?"*

Thinking about the future is helpful if it leads to pursuing higher aims or making practical plans for studies or business. However, fantasising excessively about the future can be harmful.

During a Vedanta class, my teacher Janki Santoke, a senior disciple of Swami A Parthasarathy, explained three different ways to approach our goals:

- *I do it because it makes me happy.* For instance, I love to exercise because it brings me joy, sometimes even overdoing it.

- *I do it because I want to avoid trouble.* For example, I exercise because my doctors told me to, due to diabetes.

- *I do it because it's the right thing and leads me to my goal.* For example, exercising because it is the proper way to maintain health.

Though the activity in all three scenarios is the same, the attitude (intentions) matters profoundly. The third approach captures the essence of living purposefully.

This framework and mindset will support your journey to uncover your true purpose and align your goals with what deeply matters to you. The exercise on Experiences, Contribution and Growth is a practical step to bring clarity and inspiration to this quest.

Be Patient with Yourself

Finding your life purpose is likely one of the biggest and most important questions you will ever face. It's perfectly natural for this process to take time. Your understanding of what you want and how you plan to achieve it will change and deepen over time and this evolution is an essential part of the journey.

As Janki Santoke wisely shared in a seminar on *Governing Business and Relationships* (also a book by Swami A Parthasarathy): *"Your understanding of what you want to achieve and how you'll achieve it will evolve."*

The key is to keep asking yourself these profound questions and exploring the answers that arise. In doing so, your goals and actions will align more closely with what truly matters to you, leading to a life of deeper fulfilment and purpose.

Making It Manageable and Share Your Purpose

For some, creating a clearly defined life purpose can feel overwhelming. If you struggle, try breaking it down and focus on what you want to achieve in the near future.

Sharing your purpose also amplifies its impact. When you tell others, *"This is the impact I want to have in the world,"* you declare your intention to the universe and invite support and encouragement. This shared journey helps make your purpose more real and achievable, fostering connection and motivation.

Activity – Finding Your Purpose in Life

Keep your pen and paper ready. Write down:

- What kind of experience do I want to have in my life? *(Write your experience here)*

- What kind of impact do I want to have on the world? *(Write your impact here)*

- How will I grow to have that experience and impact? *(Write your growth plan here)*

The Power of Sharing Your Purpose

When you share your purpose with friends, family, or a mentor, you strengthen your motivation and desire to become the person capable of achieving your most ambitious goals. Their encouragement can be invaluable, so don't hesitate to share your purpose today.

I look forward to guiding you through the next important steps on your journey to success!

Are You Ready to Lean into Discomfort and Grow?

Let me share a story about a student on a journey of self-discovery and personal growth. His experience with meditation reminds us of that growth often comes with discomfort and that discomfort is a necessary part of the process.

- The student narrates: *"I recently took up meditation. I wanted to strengthen my core and was slowly getting used to holding my body steady. But in today's class, my legs went numb, and my hands ached."*

- The instructor said, *"And now, keep your body steady..."*

- The student thought, *"Oh great. While everyone else became more alert and attentive, I tried to hide. My muscles quaked like a pneumatic drill. The instructor noticed, but after the meditation was over..."*

- The instructor reassured him, *"Don't worry! Let your body ache! This is where you decide if you will lean into discomfort and grow, or if you will avoid discomfort and stay exactly as you are."*

Later that day, the student reflected deeply on those words.

Reflections on Discomfort and Growth

I began to wonder, *"What if we leaned into discomfort a little more? What if we pursued it proactively instead of avoiding or dismissing the unfamiliar and uncomfortable?"*

Joseph Campbell, the American mythologist and one of my heroes, said, *"Fear, uncertainty, and discomfort are your compasses toward growth. We must let go of the planned life and accept the life waiting for us."*

Consider what you might be avoiding right now. Is it writing that email, going to that workout, applying for that job, ending a relationship, or beginning a business? Maybe you're avoiding a certain person or even avoiding happiness itself.

Could you, just for now, just as an experiment, for as long as you like, decide to lean in a little more?

When you allow discomfort to guide your growth, something incredible happens. Gifts, lessons, experiences, and opportunities seem to appear almost magically. Life shifts into an experiment where a powerful state of flow dissolves resistance.

Perhaps it's time for you to reach the next level. Perhaps it's time to lean in more. What do you think?

As Neale Donald Walsch, author of *Conversations with God,* says, "There is no coincidence, and nothing happens by accident. Each event and adventure are called to you so that you can create and experience who you are." It is no coincidence that you have arrived at these proven teachings and techniques today, as you search for your own purpose.

Chapter Summary

This chapter discusses how **purpose** shapes a meaningful life. It highlights that many goals reflect societal influences rather than personal values, and that authentic goals should come from within. The framework of **Experience, Growth, and Contribution** is introduced to help you identify what truly matters to you.

Key ideas to carry forward are:

- **Inside-out goals:** Goals imposed by society or others rarely serve your true self; authentic goals are discovered, not dictated.

- **End goals vs. means goals:** End goals focus on how you want to feel and what you want to experience, not just on material markers or stepping stones.

- **Growth as alignment:** True growth means developing skills and qualities that match your purpose and the life you genuinely wish to live.

- **Contribution as a pillar:** Purpose deepens when you ask how your experiences and growth can uplift, serve, or inspire others.

- **Evolving purpose:** Purpose is not fixed; it evolves with you, so it needs regular reflection and refinement.

- **Leaning into discomfort:** Stretch zones, where there is discomfort or uncertainty, are often where real growth lives.

- **Shared purpose:** Speaking your purpose aloud to others builds commitment, accountability, and support.

- **Purpose statement:** A clear, well-crafted purpose statement can inspire, steady, and guide your daily decisions and long-term goals.

Reflect & Apply

Use these prompts to turn the chapter into practice:

- **Map Experience, Growth, Contribution:** Write down the experiences you want, the ways you wish to grow, and how that growth can contribute to others or the world.

- **Craft your purpose statement:** Combine your unique qualities, preferred ways of expression, required growth areas, and vision of a better world into one concise statement. Keep it visible.

- **Lean into discomfort:** Identify one area you have been avoiding out of fear or uncertainty and choose one small, concrete way to lean in.

- **Share your purpose:** Discuss your evolving purpose with a trusted friend, family member, mentor, or coach to create gentle accountability and invite encouragement.

- **Schedule a purpose review:** Set a reminder, annually or even quarterly - to revisit and refine your purpose as you grow.

These insights lay the foundation for deeper self-awareness and **purposeful living.** Each small step you take toward clarity of purpose is a step toward a more authentic, fulfilling life.

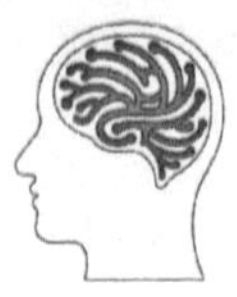

1 1

Purposeful Goal Setting

*~ Turning purpose into unstoppable goals with
VISTA and inner resources.*

Setting Out on the Journey

Nothing can stop you from achieving your goals when your purpose is clear and compelling. This chapter will help you unlock powerful mindset techniques that enable you to overcome obstacles and maintain motivation as you work towards your most meaningful aspirations, that's your purpose. This chapter is not about generic goals, but goals anchored in the purpose decoded in Chapter 10. You will discover productivity strategies to stay focused, structure your efforts, and remain on course, progressing step-by-step towards fulfilment and accomplishment.

Wisdom: Birbal and the Four Idiots

Before we proceed, let us reflect on a story that conveys important lessons about goals, purpose, and wise action. The Mughal Emperor Akbar once tasked his advisor Birbal with finding the four biggest idiots in his kingdom. After an exhaustive search, Birbal presented only two men in the court. The first had carried his own luggage on his head while riding a bullock cart, trying not to burden the bull. The second had attempted to force his cow up a ladder to graze on grass atop his hut.

Birbal explained, "Jahan Panah, searching for four idiots cost me a month of important work - I am the third. And by setting me this meaningless task, you, great King, are the fourth." Akbar laughed, realising the folly in losing sight of genuine purpose and the need to focus energy where it truly matters.

Reflections: Are Your Goals Serving Your Purpose?

This story serves as a gentle reminder: Without clear purpose and inspired goals, we risk diverting our efforts towards pursuits that do not serve our highest calling. Mindless activity, misplaced effort, or blindly following old systems leads only to unintended consequences. Wise goal setting began with purpose, focused attention, and the humility to change direction when needed.

Each step of your journey should flow from your deepest sense of purpose, not external expectations or outmoded habits. Set goals that are aligned with who you are and who you wish to become.

Building Momentum: Repeating Your Success

Every goal worth pursuing invites challenges - roadblocks, setbacks, and moments where your resolve is truly tested. But when your purpose is illuminated within, you find the drive and willpower to navigate these challenges and return to your dreams, time and again. Success is never accidental; it is a result of decisive action, clear planning, and extraordinary persistence.

True achievement is built by stacking your accomplishments, drawing inspiration from each step forward, and maintaining continuous momentum until your big goals are realised. With the right structure, support, accountability, and mental tools, any purposeful vision can be brought to life and repeated for even greater successes as your confidence grows.

From SMART to VISTA

Around 2014, drawing on my Mirror the Mind meditation practice and the DBER principle (Desire–Belief–Expectancy–Repetition), I began shaping an evolution beyond traditional SMART goals. This work grew into the VISTA model of goal setting: Visualise, Inspirational, Specific, Time-bound, Assessable – a framework designed not just to plan outcomes, but to ignite the inner state needed to achieve them.

For many years, SMART goals (Specific, Measurable, Achievable, Relevant, Time-bound) served as the standard workhorse for clarity and accountability. But times change, human aspirations deepen, and our methods must also evolve. VISTA brings in emotional energy and sensory-rich imagery so that goals are not only defined on paper but felt deeply in the heart and nervous system.

The VISTA Formula: What It Really Means

VISTA is your upgraded compass for goal setting: Visualise, Inspirational, Specific, Time-bound, Assessable. It is designed not just to plan outcomes, but to ignite the inner state that makes those outcomes possible.

- **V – Visualise.** Create a vivid mental picture of your success. Imagine how it will look, sound, feel, smell, and even taste when you reach your goal. Picture who is present, what is happening, and, most importantly, how victory feels emotionally - just as a footballer must see the goalposts or a sailor must consult a chart, your vision guides your journey.

- **I – Inspirational.** Ensure your vision genuinely moves you into action. It should not only motivate you at the finish line but also inspire you at every stage, energising your efforts so that each step forward feels meaningful.

- **S – Specific.** Define every detail needed to reach your desired outcome. Go beyond vague ambition to a precise roadmap: locations, timings, actions, and measurable qualities. Clarity about what you want and how you will get there builds confidence.

- **T – Time-bound.** Attach realistic yet stretching deadlines to your overall goal and each milestone. A time frame turns a wish into a commitment, creating urgency, momentum, and personal accountability.

- **A – Assessable.** Make your progress tangible and measurable. Break your goal into clear checkpoints - numbers, dates, or visible results and celebrate every win, no matter how small, so you can say with certainty, "Yes, I am on track."

When you structure your path with VISTA, you combine inner inspiration with outer structure, progressing steadily in ways that uplift your own life and positively impact the lives of others.

Example: "I visualise myself speaking at the national conference in October, feeling confident on stage and inspiring the audience with my story. I submit my application by March, prepare my slides by August, rehearse at least ten times by September, and celebrate each milestone as I move toward sharing my message with hundreds."

VISTA Goal-Setting

1. Visualise

- What is your vivid mental image of the goal achieved?
- How will it look, sound, smell, and feel?
- Who will be there, what will be happening, and how will you feel emotionally?
- Write your vision in present tense as if it is already real.

Example:
I see myself standing on stage at the annual conference, confidently delivering my talk to an engaged audience. The room is filled with the sound of applause and encouragement. I feel proud and inspired.

2. Inspirational

- Why does this goal inspire you?
- Does your vision excite you and motivate you to take action?
- Does imagining each step make you feel energised to proceed?

Example:
Speaking at the conference inspires me because I want to share my story and motivate others to pursue personal growth. The thought of making an impact on others fills me with enthusiasm.

3. Specific

- What exactly do you want to achieve? Be as detailed as possible.
- Which steps must you take to reach your goal?
- What are the smaller achievements that make up the journey?
- List all details: location, timing, actions, and any measurable qualities.

Example:
By next October, I will submit my speaker application, prepare a compelling presentation, rehearse ten times, and deliver a 20-minute talk at the conference.

4. Time-bound

- What is your deadline for the overall goal?

- Set deadlines for each step or milestone.

- How will you ensure you stay accountable to your time frame?

Example:
Application submitted by March; slides prepared by August; final rehearsal by September; talk delivered in October.

5. Assessable

- What progress markers or checkpoints will you use to measure success along the way?

- How will you celebrate or acknowledge these achievements?

- Make each step quantifiable: dates, numbers, or visible outcomes.

Example:
You might set milestones such as completing your application by March, finalising and submitting your slides in August, finishing all rehearsals by September, and delivering your talk in October. At each stage, acknowledge your progress with a small celebration – perhaps treating yourself to your favourite coffee, taking time for reflection, sharing your achievement with a friend, or noting your feelings in a journal. By marking these milestones in measurable ways and celebrating each one, you create a clear and motivating path toward your goal.

VISTA Goal-Setting Framework – Visualise, Inspirational, Specific, Time-bound, Assessable – ©2026 Capt. Pratap Mehta. All rights reserved.

Mindful Goal Setting: Mirror the Mind

See Appendix 3: Goal Setting and Spiritual Guides

Guided Meditation – Mirror the Mind

Mindful goal setting begins with an inner shift, not just a new to-do list. This programme guides you through achieving any goal, no matter how large:

first defining your extraordinary life and true purpose, then choosing goals aligned with that purpose and clearing inner obstacles that slow you down. As you learn to "mirror the mind," you programme your thoughts, emotions, and beliefs to support the future you want to create.

With the Mirror the Mind process, you can set clear, compelling goals and objectives, heal yourself from limiting beliefs, help support the healing of others, harness the energy of desire, and bring projects to life and fruition.

Take Control of Your Life

There is an old saying: let nothing hold you back from creating the life you have always wanted. One of the most profound discoveries you will ever make is the untapped potential of your mind. Ask yourself: do you take charge of your life, or do external circumstances dictate how your story unfolds? Let these questions settle within as we prepare to explore how your mind can help you achieve what you truly desire.

The Power of Sharing Your Purpose

Sharing your purpose with others amplifies its power. When you tell people, "This is the impact I want to have in the world," the universe and the people around you often conspire to support that intention. Your goals gain momentum, and help appears in surprising ways - through opportunities, introductions, and insights that arrive just when you need them.

Many Small Goals, One Purpose

To fulfil a big life purpose, you will usually pursue many smaller goals along the way. Each completed goal is a victory and a message to your subconscious that you are capable and moving in the right direction. Using mindful techniques to mirror your thoughts and intentions, you can steadily achieve these goals while keeping them aligned with your deepest "why."

Mindful Meditation Process: Mirror the Mind

Begin by visualising a large mental screen, like a giant TV - about six to ten feet in front of you, slightly above your eye level. When you gently close your eyes and raise your gaze about 20 degrees, you stimulate your brain's alpha wave activity, making it easier to relax and connect with your inner mind.

With this mental screen in place, choose a goal aligned with your purpose. It might be:

- A new relationship

- Better health

- A new home

- A dream career

Picture this goal as vividly as you can. If you are new to mindful meditation, choose a goal you aim to achieve within three years. Stretch your imagination and ask yourself:

- What will that ideal relationship feel like?

- How will your ideal body look and feel?

- What would your ideal home be like?

- What does your dream career look like day to day?

Imagine yourself on that mental screen fully experiencing your goal and take a few moments to immerse yourself in this vision.

Cultivate Strong Willpower: DBER

To achieve anything meaningful, you need intense, focused willpower, which can be trained through the DBER principle:

- **D – Desire**

- **B – Belief**

- **E – Expectancy**

- **R – Repetition**

When clear desire, deep belief, confident expectancy, and consistent repetition come together, your mind becomes a powerful ally in turning purposeful goals into reality.

Faith, Focus, and Following Through

Umbrella in the Desert: Power of Belief

My brother-in-law, Ajit Mehta, IAS, who served as Desert Commissioner at Jodhpur, once shared a powerful tale from a severe drought in Jaisalmer in the late 1980s. During a community Havan, where he was the Chief Guest, people had gathered anxiously to pray for rain. As the rituals began, a young boy named Shyam Singh walked in carrying an umbrella – a quiet, unforgettable symbol of his deep belief and expectancy that the rains would come, despite the scorching, cloudless sky.

Success Is Not a One-Off Event

When you programme your mind in the Alpha state, your faith combined with strong DBER – Desire, Belief, Expectancy, Repetition – helps you heal, learn, and manifest what you truly seek. Achieving a goal once or twice might be coincidence, but sustained success comes from a repeatable inner process that preserves and builds on your mental programming, instead of starting from zero each time.

Alpha Activator: Three-Finger Anchoring

You will now learn a technique called Three-Finger Anchoring, or Alpha Activator. This simple physical cue allows you to recall your pre-programmed mind and quickly enter your Alpha state – your inner, subconscious space – anytime and anywhere. By gently bringing three fingers together, you trigger a state of focus, calm, and inner power that helps you address challenges more effectively.

Dream Big: One Life-Changing Goal

Now, imagine achieving one big, life-changing goal before the end of this year. What would that be, and what accomplishment would fill you with pride, joy, fulfilment, and gratitude? Know this: when your mind is aligned and your methods are clear, that goal is completely achievable.

Why Most Fail – and How You Won't

Only a small fraction of people who make New Year's resolutions actually succeed, yet those who set clear resolutions are still far more likely to reach their goals than those who never start. Most people fail not because their dreams are wrong, but because they lack tools, support, and a realistic plan; they attempt too much too quickly, feel overwhelmed, and lose motivation.

The Arrow and the Archer

An ancient tale speaks of an archer famed for his unerring accuracy. When a young boy asked, "How do you always hit your target?" the archer replied, "I do not focus on the arrow; I fix my gaze firmly on the target. The arrow follows my vision; it knows where to go." When the boy tried focusing on the arrow instead of the target, he repeatedly missed, until the archer explained that true power lies in unwavering focus on the goal, not on the means.

Reflections: Purpose as Your True Target

This story reminds us that in goal setting, clarity of purpose is paramount: your vision – the unwavering mental image of what you deeply desire, acts as your compass. If you fixate on every obstacle or minor step ("the arrow"), your aim can waver and your energy scatter; when your purpose is clear and your goals align with it, obstacles become secondary and your efforts harmonise.

Goal setting is not just about ticking off tasks; it is a conscious, mindful process powered by clarity, intention, and inspired action. Your purpose is your target – keep your gaze on it, and let your goals follow, so your journey remains steady, inspired, and full of growth, guided like an arrow by the light of that inner aim.

Your Path Forward

From here, you will learn how to choose a purpose aligned with your highest vision, create a realistic step-by-step action plan, and use mindset tools to stay motivated as you advance towards that purpose. With a clear "why" and a solid plan, you can maintain momentum through every challenge and begin working with the Visualisation Zone, where your inner resources and spiritual guides come alive to support your journey.

Visualisation Zone & Spiritual Guides

See Appendix 3: Goal Setting and Spiritual Guides

Guided Meditation – Visualisation Zone and Spiritual Guides

The Visualisation Zone is a focused inner space where you direct your mind's attention and become deeply aware of powerful inner imagery. In this state, your visualisation and imagination come alive, engaging all your senses – colour, brightness, texture, temperature, smell, taste, sound, rhythm, and motion; use the VAK (Visual, Auditory, Kinaesthetic) techniques from earlier chapters to enrich this experience.

Your mind is an extraordinary creator, capable of generating "coincidences," opening doors of opportunity, and shaping what appears as "luck" to guide you toward your goals. In essence, you are learning to use the power of thought intentionally to influence your reality.

Avoiding the Pitfalls of Visualisation

Many people fall into a subtle trap: they visualise the wrong goals or chase opportunities that are misaligned with their true selves. How many wake up in jobs they dislike, pursuing dreams that no longer resonate? To avoid this, you work at the Alpha level of your mind. The subconscious space where clear insight emerges – allows this process to flood your awareness with ideas, guidance, and solutions to challenges that once felt insurmountable.

Through such inner work, you begin to discover your true mission and align your goals with your authentic life purpose. Everyone's mission is unique – raising remarkable children, writing a transformative book, saving the rainforests, launching businesses, or empowering communities. To support this journey, you will learn to create two powerful inner spaces: the Resource Gateway and the Resource Centre, portals to positive energy and inner resources that sustain your progress.

Resource Gateway

Begin by passing through the Resource Gateway, a mental threshold connecting you to the full spectrum of your inner strengths and energies. As you move through this gateway, you become aware of various positive energy patterns, including:

- Physical resources: poise, posture, strength, vitality
- Emotional resources: courage, compassion, resilience

- Intellectual resources: clarity, wisdom, discernment

- Intuitive and spiritual resources: intuition, healing energy, creativity, oneness, and sense of purpose

Crossing this gateway prepares your mind and body to receive guidance and inspiration, reinforcing your inner stability and motivation for the path ahead.

Your Inner Resource Centre

Once you pass through the Gateway, you enter your Inner Resource Centre – a personal sanctuary crafted by your mind in a deeply relaxed state. This centre has no limits except those you imagine and is designed to encourage creative thinking and effective problem-solving.

Furnish your Resource Centre in ways that support focus and inspiration, for example:

- A comfortable chair to rest and reflect

- A desk or table for planning and creating

- A time mechanism representing past, present, and future

- A replicator or photocopier to "duplicate" ideas

- A laptop and printer for your work and connections

- A mental screen or TV to visualise and manifest projects

- A medicine chest or toolbox for healing and strength

- Chairs for your male and female intuitive consultants or spiritual guides

Intuitive Consultants or Spiritual Guides

Within your Resource Centre, your Intuitive Consultants or Spiritual Guides act as wise allies who boost your confidence, motivation, and inspiration. Whenever you face a challenge or need creative insight, you can approach them in your mind's eye and imagine them offering advice, fresh perspectives, or illuminating solutions.

Create your male and female consultants thoughtfully; they represent higher intelligence and genius and should remain unchanged for up to six months to build deep trust. For personal issues, consult the corresponding guide (male issues with the male guide, female issues with the female guide), and allow these inner figures to become ongoing sources of encouragement and direction.

Using the Resource Gateway and Alpha State

To enter your Resource Centre:

- Take three deep breaths to relax.

- Count down slowly from 10 to 1 as you mentally pass through the Resource Gateway.

- Greet your consultants and ask clearly for the guidance or insight you need.

- When your session is complete, return awareness gently to the present, feeling refreshed and empowered.

Visual-oriented people often notice vivid images, while auditory-oriented people may pick up inner sounds and tones more clearly; both styles are equally valid and powerful.

Tips for Effective Programming

You can programme your Alpha Activator for specific events or situations the night before they occur; for example, students can visit their consultant and request help in recalling information during an exam. Apply any Mind Power Technique from the Appendix to address challenges such as insomnia, time management, headaches, intuitive problem-solving, skill rehearsal, and goal setting.

When practised at the Alpha (subconscious) level, three-finger actuators combined with affirmations become exponentially more powerful than when used in the normal waking state. Always close your session with gratitude and a deliberate return to full awareness, feeling renewed and filled with vitality. If the Alpha Activator does not seem to work at times, it may signal that you are not yet ready to pursue that goal, that you are being protected from loss or risk, or simply that you need more practice with the technique.

How to Ask Your Intuitive Guides

There is no rigid ritual for asking your Intuitive Consultants or Spiritual Guides for help; what matters is that you *consciously ask*. You can speak your request out loud, hold the question clearly in your mind, direct it to your guide during meditation, or write it down - use whatever method feels natural and sincere.

Your guides are always near, communicating through ideas, impressions, and intuition, but you retain full free will to accept or ignore their guidance. Because free will is fundamental, they will not interfere with your decisions or actions unless invited, which is why it is essential to ask for their input deliberately. When you do, ask precise, clear questions, remembering that your guides will not spoonfeed answers, predict exact outcomes, give simple yes/no responses, or reveal information you are not yet ready to receive.

Instead, they support and encourage you by offering insights that help you get "unstuck," while the responsibility to act on that guidance always remains yours. After asking, stay open to guidance in many forms: a timely conversation, a book passage, a sign, a song, a memory, or even a digital prompt that speaks directly to your situation. The key is to remain open and to trust your experiences; when you sense communication from your guides, acknowledge it, and when it passes, consciously express gratitude. Practising this loop of Asking, Acknowledgment, and Gratitude gradually deepens your connection with your Intuitive Spiritual Guides.

Let me share a closing story.

The Sage and the Silent Guides

Long ago, a young seeker approached a renowned sage, yearning to find guidance for his life's purpose. The sage took him to a quiet forest and said, "Close your eyes and listen - not with your ears but with your heart. Around you are silent guides waiting to speak."

The seeker sat patiently, but no words came. Frustrated, he asked, "Master, how do I hear their guidance if they do not speak?"

The sage smiled, "Our greatest guides do not shout or command. They whisper through intuition, symbols, feelings, and sudden clarity. Like the subtle rustle in the trees or the gentle warmth of the sun on your skin, their messages arrive softly, waiting for an open heart to receive them."

Reflections: Trusting Subtle Guidance

This story reminds us that intuitive guides - whether inner wisdom, spiritual helpers, or creative insight, often communicate in subtle, gentle ways rather than loud or obvious commands.

To connect with these guides, we must cultivate stillness and receptivity.

Guidance manifests through feelings, chance meetings, thoughts, dreams, or unexpected signs.

The true power lies in trust - trusting your intuition, trusting the soft nudges of your subconscious, and acting upon the messages you receive.

Like the seeker, patience and openness are key to hearing and following your guides.

Our spiritual and intuitive guides support us on our path, ready to inspire, encourage, and illuminate our journey. When you listen carefully, you will find that the answers you seek are closer than you imagine.

Remember, without purpose, when we go mindlessly on our way, creating more unintended consequences and failing to achieve anything worthwhile, we have no right to blame anyone but ourselves for the consequences. Therefore, your goals must be the outcome of your purpose.

Chapter Summary

This chapter explores how goal setting becomes truly transformational when it is anchored in clear purpose, a vivid inner vision, and mindful techniques. It shows how a strong inner picture of success fuels motivation, helps you navigate obstacles, and supports steady progress toward goals that actually matter to your life's mission.

Key ideas to carry forward are:

- **Purpose-powered vision:** A clear vision aligned with your highest purpose is the foundation of sustained, unstoppable achievement.

- **From SMART to VISTA:** The **VISTA** framework (Visualise, Inspirational, Specific, Time-bound, Assessable) goes beyond SMART by adding emotional energy and vivid, measurable progress.

- **Multi-sensory visualisation:** Engaging all five senses makes your goals emotionally compelling, driving consistent effort.

- **Inner Resource Gateway & Centre:** Creating an inner sanctuary gives you conscious access to physical, emotional, intellectual, and spiritual strengths that support your success.

- **Intuitive Consultants / Spiritual Guides:** These inner allies offer insight, warning, and encouragement, especially in challenging times.

- **Working in Alpha:** Mind power techniques practised in the relaxed Alpha (subconscious) state are far more effective than those used only in the normal waking state.

- **Gratitude to your Guides:** Regularly asking, acknowledging, and thanking your Intuitive Guides deepens your inner support system.

- **Celebrate milestones:** Marking each assessable step reinforces motivation and keeps your progress visible and satisfying.

Reflect & Apply

Use these prompts to bring the chapter from concept to practice:

Clarify your vision: Draw a vivid mental picture of your ultimate goal. What do you see, hear, feel, and experience when it is achieved?

- **Use VISTA to shape goals:** Break your goals into inspirational, specific, time-bound, and assessable steps, with clear deadlines for each.

- **Create your Resource Gateway and Centre:** Through mindful meditation, build an inner sanctuary where your strengths, wisdom, and intuition are easy to access.

- **Connect with your Intuitive Guides:** Practise asking clearly for guidance, stay open to different channels of insight, and cultivate gratitude for every nudge and synchronicity.

- **Apply mind power in Alpha:** Experiment with relaxed, meditative states for goal setting, healing, problem-solving, and skill mastery.

Together, these practices offer a holistic approach that blends **practical action planning with inner self-empowerment**, enabling you to realise goals that genuinely align with your life's purpose.

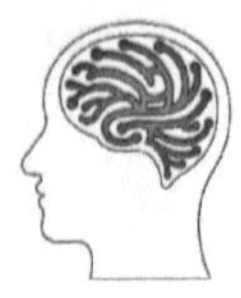

1 2

Law of Attraction

~ Harnessing the law of effortless success.

Perspective on Manifesting Desires

Many people have been intrigued by the idea that the universe mirrors back our wishes, and that manifesting our desires requires little more than strong determination, a few choice words, and faith in the cosmic rhythm. While there is truth in this concept, real manifestation begins with a thorough understanding of its origins and the right ways to align ourselves with this powerful law. Let's embark on a journey into the fascinating realm of manifestation, an ancient practice that enables us to fulfil our deepest desires. But where did this concept originate?

The origins of the Law of Attraction are frequently attributed to Hinduism. As one of the world's most ancient religions, Hinduism has provided a substantial foundation of spiritual teachings and is notable for its early references to the concepts of manifestation through concentrated thought and intention. Let me share a real-life experience from my Navy days.

The Bridge Watch That Drew the Flagship Back

During Exercise South Paw, a major Western Fleet exercise in the Arabian Sea, I was officer of the watch (OOW) on the middle watch on the bridge of INS Rajput. The night was a classic monsoon cocktail - driving rain, heavy swell, and thick fog rolling across the formation. The Flag of the Western Fleet was flying on board INS Deepak, our replenishment tanker and flagship for the exercise.

At one point, our surface picture on radar degraded and we briefly lost a firm contact on Deepak's echo in the clutter. For a few tense moments, the flagship's precise bearing and range were uncertain, even though the formation was meant to be maintaining station on her. Visibility was almost zero, radar screen speckled with rain clutter, and every officer on the bridge felt the unspoken question. Captain unperturbed, remained seated in his Chair.

In that instant, I centred myself, took a slow breath, and closed my eyes for a heartbeat. I *visualised* Deepak clearly steady on base course, making good way, exactly where she was supposed to be, our formation closed up correctly around the guide. No panic, only clear intent: *She's ahead. We're in proper station. The Fleet is intact.* When I opened my eyes, the radar screen (PPI) stabilised, the flagship's echo came back clean on the correct bearing and range, and moments later her calm voice came on the circuit confirming her position.

Captain S. W. Lakhkar, then in command of INS Rajput, later commended my composure and presence of mind in handling the situation without excitement or confusion on the bridge. For me, that night became more than a good Officer Of the Watch story - it was a living demonstration of the Law of Attraction at sea. My focused thought and feeling aligned with the reality we needed, and the picture resolved to match that inner clarity.

Reflections – Essence of Manifesting Desires

This is the essence of the Law of Attraction: what you consistently think about, speak about, hold firm beliefs about, and feel deeply about, you begin to draw into your experience. Applied correctly, it can be as real on a dark, rolling bridge wing as it is in any meditation hall.

Having personally applied the Law of Attraction to achieve significant milestones in both my life and Navy career, I have seen it work wonders. Yet, paradoxically, it doesn't work for everyone. The challenge isn't with the law itself; it lies in how individuals apply, or sometimes misapply, these teachings. Small, innocent-seeming mistakes can severely limit results and sometimes prevent any success altogether.

At its core, the Law of Attraction states: *What you think about, speak about, hold firm beliefs about, and feel deeply about, you will bring into your life.* This truth has been echoed by some of history's greatest minds and spiritual teachers, reminding us how our inner mental landscape shapes our outer reality.

Consider These Timeless Insights

- "What things soever ye desire, when ye pray, believe that ye receive them, and ye shall have them." — Mark 11:24 (King James Bible)

- "All that we are is a result of what we have thought." — Buddha

- "A man is but the product of his thoughts. What he thinks he becomes." — Mahatma Gandhi

- "The empires of the future are the empires of the mind." — Winston Churchill

- "We become what we think about all day long." — Ralph Waldo Emerson

- "Until you make the unconscious conscious, it will direct your life, and you will call it fate." — Carl Jung

- "Surely Allah does not change the condition of a people until they change what is in themselves." — Quran 13:11

- "The mind alone is the friend of the self, and the mind alone is the enemy of the self." — Bhagavad Gita Ch6:V5

These scriptures and luminaries understood that our thoughts exert profound control over our lives, shaping not only what we possess but also our entire experience and place in the world.

Are Thoughts Really Energy?

Modern science confirms an astonishing reality: everything in the universe, tangible or intangible, is composed of energy. From towering buildings to fragrant flowers, every physical object is made of billions of microscopic atoms, dynamic energy packets interacting in complex ways.

Similarly, our thoughts - though intangible, are energy forms that influence and interact with the physical world. Brainwaves, the measurable energy of our mental activity, can be detected with medical technology and affect physical states.

What does this mean in everyday terms? Have you ever thought of a friend, moments before they call? Or intensely desired something for months and suddenly found it arriving through unexpected channels? These are examples of your thoughts and desires sending out energy signals, aligning circumstances and opportunities in response.

For example, someone consistently visualising career success may find themselves more confident and decisive in interviews, creating a positive feedback loop that furthers their goals.

Vibrational Foundation of Attraction

The Law of Attraction operates on the principle that everything vibrates at a certain frequency. Our thoughts and emotions emit energy vibrations - positive thoughts radiate higher frequencies, while negative emotions lower them.

By consciously focusing on positive thoughts and uplifting emotions, you elevate your vibrational frequency, aligning yourself with the energy of what you desire, thus attracting those outcomes into your life.

Albert Einstein famously said: *"The world as we have created it, is a process of our thinking. It cannot be changed without changing our thinking."*

This reminds us that transformation begins in the mind, with deliberate shifts in how we think and feel.

Mastering The Law of Attraction

Mastering the Law of Attraction means using deliberate, disciplined thought to shape your reality through a simple three-step process: Ask, Believe, and Receive. This is the essence of the law of intention - directing your inner world so the outer world can respond in kind. (Adapted from a seminar by Jack Canfield.)

Step One: Ask

Ask for What You Want, Not What You Fear

Each day, you send hundreds of "requests" to both the universe and your subconscious mind through what you think, read, watch, say, and dwell on. The articles you consume, the programmes you binge, the social media you scroll, the music you play, all of it feeds your inner vibration. When this mental activity is random, negative, or unfocused, you unintentionally programme yourself for lack, limitation, and struggle.

Criticising yourself, complaining about circumstances, or obsessing over what is missing keeps your attention locked on what you do not want. Blaming, fault-finding, or judging others does the same, anchoring your energy to problems instead of possibilities. Worrying is simply negative goal setting: you build vivid internal pictures of outcomes you dread, and your energy begins to align with those scenarios. The Law of Attraction responds not to your wishes, but to where your attention, emotion, and belief consistently rest.

Thoughts as Vibration

Every thought and feeling you generate carries a distinct vibrational frequency, whether you are aware of it or not. Most people live in constant reaction - responding emotionally to news headlines, market swings, messages, and other people's behaviour, without ever pausing to decide what they *truly* want to experience. When you live this way, you remain "stuck" in a loop where life keeps reflecting back the same patterns.

In contrast, when your inner state is enthusiastic, joyful, grateful, loving, relaxed, and appreciative, you radiate elevated vibrations. Negative emotions such as anxiety, confusion, sadness, frustration, or chronic stress lower your frequency and attract more of the same quality of experience. Becoming conscious of your emotional climate is the first step to asking clearly.

Start Intentionally Creating Your Future

To move from passive reactor to intentional creator, you must first decide what you want and then practise feeling the emotions of already having it.

Perhaps you want to change your career, move to a new city, earn recognition, appear on television, or heal from illness. Ask yourself: *If this were already true, how would I feel? How would I spend my day? Who would be around me?* The more your thoughts and conversations revolve around what you *do* want, rather than what you want to avoid, the faster your reality begins to shift in that direction.

Imagine your mind as an inner GPS. Each clearly imagined outcome, each sincere preference, is like typing a destination into that system. Whether you desire a table by the window, front-row tickets, a restorative holiday, or a deeply loving partnership, every specific intention is a clear instruction to the universe about where you wish to go.

Utilise Language That Promotes Progress

The words you choose to describe your life are powerful signals. Instead of reinforcing lack with statements like, "I want to get out of debt," you can affirm, "I am living a life of abundance and wealth." Language that points toward the desired state trains your mind and emotions to align with it. Maintaining a positive outlook, speaking with expectancy, and framing your goals as already in motion is one of the most effective ways to *ask* the universe for what you truly desire.

Replace Negative Pictures with Empowering Ones

Much like an author shapes a story, you have the power to shape your future by deliberately focusing on the images and outcomes you want to experience. When faced with challenges, avoid fuelling negativity through repeated talk, complaints, or replaying problems in your mind. If you catch yourself worrying, intentionally shift your attention to imagining the best possible results - see, hear, and feel those positive scenarios in detail. This purposeful daydreaming demonstrates the principle of visualisation.

If you find you're judging yourself or criticising others, notice that your thoughts are drifting toward what you don't want. Pause gently, break the cycle, and refocus on your true choices. Mindfulness, meditation, and being present are important tools; they provide the awareness and space needed to change your focus and, ultimately, steer your future in a positive direction.

Ask Clearly, Then Let the Universe Orchestrate

Your role is to clarify and sustain your desire, not to control the entire mechanism of how it will be fulfilled. Do not overload yourself with the "how"; that is the universe's domain. When you become clear about what you want and consistently focus your energy, attention, and emotion on that outcome, you become magnetic to people, resources, and events that resonate with your intention.

Like a GPS finding efficient routes with a clear destination, life aligns in unexpected ways when your intentions are definite. This principle of manifestation goes beyond religion and resonates with anyone committed to pursuing their highest goals.

Step One is your declaration. In the next step, you learn how to Believe - aligning your faith and actions so that what you have asked for can move towards you.

Step Two: Believe

Believe You'll Achieve Your Goals and Act Accordingly

Believing you'll get what you want means living each day with genuine hope and quiet certainty, trusting that your future is guided by forces greater than yourself. It's about choosing, with solid conviction, to see your goals as achievable realities. Achieving this kind of faith isn't always easy.

Many people struggle with limiting beliefs that quietly block their path to happiness and abundance. If this resonates with you, remember that the first change begins within: gradually replace old, unhelpful thoughts with ones that assure you are deserving, capable, lovable, valuable, and "enough" in every meaningful way. When your mindset aligns with your aspirations, action is the next step.

Taking real steps shows both you and the universe that you believe in your dreams. These actions might be clear - like signing up for medical courses if you want to become a doctor or changing your diet for better health. Such practical measures are available right now; you don't have to wait for a magical moment. Consistent effort is key, the universe responds to those who move forward with purpose.

Sometimes, action comes from intuition - a sudden idea or urge you can't quite explain. You might feel drawn to reach out to someone or attend an event unexpectedly. While you may not know exactly how everything fits together, trust in your vision lets you follow these instincts and watch future steps reveal themselves, almost as if by magic.

Recognising Moments for Inspired Action

When you work with the Law of Attraction, you'll notice that fresh ideas and inspiration start appearing more often - perhaps during meditation or quiet moments. Opportunities might show up as a well-timed phone call, a financial boost, or an unexpected meeting, sometimes exactly when you need it. These inspired thoughts aren't random; they are signs from the universe guiding you toward your goals because you're aligned with your intentions.

It's important to stay aware and open-minded. When opportunity knocks, seize it quickly, taking advantage of the positive energy. Simply thinking positively isn't enough - it's action that transforms possibilities into reality.

As Wallace D. Wattles, author of *The Science of Getting Rich*, put it: *"By thought, the thing you want is brought to you; by action, you receive it."*

Step Three: Receive

Align Your Vibration to Receive What You Want

Everything in existence vibrates at a particular frequency, including your thoughts and emotions. To genuinely receive what you seek, you must become a "vibrational match" for your desire. Think of yourself as a radio set: if you want to hear jazz, you must tune to the jazz frequency, not heavy metal. In the same way, if you wish to attract abundance, health, love, or peace, your inner state needs to resonate with those very qualities.

One of the simplest ways to do this is to consciously generate elevated emotions - love, joy, appreciation, and gratitude, throughout your day. Imagine yourself already living the reality you want and practise feeling the emotions that would naturally arise from it. Because thoughts generate feelings, you must watch your inner dialogue carefully. When you notice "I cannot afford the mortgage" or "This will never work," gently shift to more empowering alternatives such as "I will find a way," while picturing yourself meeting those commitments with ease and confidence. At first this may feel artificial, but with repetition it becomes a supportive habit that aligns your energy with your chosen outcome.

Shape Your Frequency with Affirmations

Affirmations are precise tools for re-aligning thought and emotion. An affirmation is a clear, positive statement of your goal, framed in the present as though it is already unfolding. Write your affirmations down and repeat them regularly, allowing them to soak into your subconscious mind until images and feelings of success become familiar territory.

Combine affirmations with vivid visualisation. See your goal as accomplished and hold yourself in the emotional state that would accompany that success. Be mindful, however: resentment, envy, or frustration about what you do not yet have create a vibrational clash and slow manifestation. It is extremely difficult to attract your deepest desires while carrying bitterness or harsh self-judgement; these states push your dreams away instead of inviting them closer. As Meister Eckhart observed, "If the only prayer you ever say in your entire life is *thank you*, it would be enough."

Cultivate Alignment Through Appreciation and Gratitude

Two of the fastest emotions for raising your vibration are appreciation and gratitude. If your desire were already fulfilled, you would naturally feel grateful - so you can begin practising that gratitude *now*, ahead of the physical result. Doing so magnetises more experiences that match that feeling.

Make this a daily discipline. Set aside five or ten quiet minutes to focus on what you appreciate - people, opportunities, lessons, comforts, even challenges that helped you grow. Write a short gratitude list in your journal; this simple act can shift your emotional state more powerfully than you might expect.

Try "appreciation meditation" by silently noting anything that brings comfort or joy, from simple sensations to the work behind them. This practice often boosts happiness, reduces stress, and fosters an environment for dreams to grow.

Vedic Perspective on Manifesting Desires

Vedic Roots of the Law of Attraction

Many trace the Law of Attraction back to the wisdom streams of Hinduism and with good reason. Hindu philosophy is anchored in the Vedas, the ancient sacred texts that form the bedrock of India's spiritual knowledge. Among these, the Rig Veda is considered the oldest, dating at least to around 1500 BCE, and possibly much earlier according to several scholars. Despite their antiquity, the Vedas offer remarkably practical guidance for living a moral, successful, and harmonious life, emphasising disciplines like yoga, meditation, and self-mastery to align oneself with the larger order of the universe.

Within this tradition, some of the earliest ideas about manifestation appear. The Brihadaranyaka Upanishad, composed around the 2nd century BCE, teaches that the cosmos itself is shaped by the mind and that Atman - the true Self, is intimately one with Brahman, the cosmic Self. German Indologist Paul Deussen highlights how this text famously proclaims: "As a man thinks in his heart, so is he." This insight mirrors the modern Law of Attraction: our dominant thoughts and feelings are generative forces, actively co-creating our reality. To manifest something, we must think and feel as though it is already present; our inner state quietly sets the boundaries of what can enter our lives.

Bhagavad Gita's Perspective on Manifesting Desires

The Bhagavad Gita, one of India's most revered scriptures, agrees that thoughts shape experience but adds a crucial refinement: true manifestation arises from *clear intention plus selfless action, held with detachment from results.* Lord Krishna instructs Arjuna to first clarify his desires and purpose, then to act wholeheartedly, offering his work to the Divine while releasing anxiety about outcomes. In simple terms: do your best and surrender the rest to Higher.

This is the essence of Karma Yoga, the "yoga of action" - fulfilling one's duties as a sacred offering, without clinging to success or fearing failure. To Such surrender loosens the grip of ego and aligns the individual with a larger universal harmony. The Gita encapsulates the power of sustained thought in Chapter 8, Verse 6:*"Of whatever being one thinks at the end, while leaving the body, to that alone one goes, O Kunteya (Arjuna), because of constantly thinking of that being during his lifetime."*

As Janki Santoke, a senior disciple of Swami Parthasarathy notes, a person's final thoughts are simply the sum of countless prior reflections; the mind's trajectory cannot be changed in a moment.

If a person spends a lifetime absorbed in base, purely material desires, he is naturally drawn to similar patterns in future experiences. Both the Gita and the Law of Attraction therefore converge on a single principle: your predominant thoughts become your destiny, so nurturing positive, focused intentions - regardless of external conditions, is essential.

Meditation is upheld in this tradition as a supreme tool for aligning thought, emotion, and intention. Through steady practice of presence, self-awareness, compassion, and non-attachment, you cultivate an inner field where genuine peace and joy can arise, allowing you to attract not just what you *want*, but what truly serves your soul's evolution.

Chapter Summary

This chapter explores the Law of Attraction as a profound, time-tested principle found in ancient wisdom, especially the Vedas and the Bhagavad Gita. Mastery of this law means aligning your inner vibration with what you wish to experience through clear intention, elevated emotions, affirmations, gratitude, and mindful awareness.

Key ideas to carry forward are:

- **Intention shapes destiny:** What you consistently think and feel becomes the blueprint of your future.

- **Energy follows thought:** Your thoughts and emotions emit subtle energy that interacts with the world around you.

- **Focus is a magnet:** Dwelling on what you fear or dislike attracts more of the same; focusing on what you truly desire draws it closer.

- **Practical tools:** Visualisation, affirmations, and gratitude are simple, daily ways to raise your vibrational frequency.

- **Inspired action:** Intuitive nudges and inner guidance must be honoured alongside logical, practical effort.

- **Detachment:** As the Bhagavad Gita teaches, acting wholeheartedly while releasing anxiety about results keeps you peaceful and aligned.

- **Inner practice:** Regular meditation and mindfulness cultivate the clarity, balance, and emotional stability needed for effective manifestation.

Reflect and Apply

Use these questions and practices to bring the law from theory into life:

- **Reflect:** Notice recurring thoughts or emotional loops that may be blocking your desires. Are you feeding fear and frustration, or hope and possibility?

- **Affirm:** Write daily affirmations that state your goals as already true, such as "I am living a life of abundance" or "I move confidently towards my dreams."

- **Practise gratitude:** Each day, list a few things you genuinely appreciate and observe how your mood and outlook shift.

- **Act on intuition:** When a gentle inner nudge suggests a call, a step, or a change, act promptly and watch how the path unfolds.

- **Meditate regularly:** Set aside time for mindfulness or meditation to strengthen presence and reduce attachment to outcomes.

- **Set clear goals:** Define precisely what you want to manifest so your inner "GPS" knows where to guide you.

By weaving these practices into your routine, you move from wishing to consciously co-creating a life aligned with your deepest aspirations and highest good.

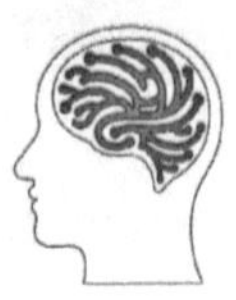

13

Mental Health Unmasked

~ Courage, Care, and Conscious Healing

Why Mental Health

Mental health is no longer a side-topic; it is the foundation on which everything else in our lives rests - parenting, teaching, leadership, relationships, even our spiritual growth. When we, as parents and educators, commit to our own inner growth and to nurturing the minds of our children, we become far better equipped to serve families, organisations, and society at large. World Mental Health Day, observed every year on 10 October since 1992, is a reminder to pause, reflect, and ask: *How well are we really caring for our inner world?*

Before stepping into the science and spirituality of mental health, consider this simple village tale of a donkey in a well.

Shake It Off and Step Up

Once upon a time, a farmer's donkey fell into a deep, dry well. The terrified animal cried for hours while the farmer and neighbours debated what to do. Eventually the farmer, deciding the donkey was old and the well needed covering anyway, asked everyone to start shovelling dirt into the well, assuming this was the end.

But the donkey responded differently. With each shovelful of dirt landing on his back, he shook it off and stepped up. Shovel after shovel, shake after shake, step after step, he rose higher until, to everyone's astonishment, he simply stepped out of the well and walked away with dignity.

Reflections – Metaphor for Resilience & Emotional Hygiene

It is more than a children's story; it is a metaphor for resilience, emotional hygiene, and the daily choice to respond rather than collapse. The donkey's act of "shaking off and stepping up" mirrors exactly what good mental health demands from us: not the absence of dirt or difficulty, but the courage to use every shovelful life throws at us as a step higher - physically, emotionally, and mentally.

Life, too, will throw "dirt" at you - criticism, stress, loss, rejection, and invisible pressures on your mind. When that happens, you have a choice: stay buried or shake it off and step up. Your nervous system and mind are designed to move through ups and downs; no special equipment is needed, just the willingness to take one small step at a time. Good mental health is not a distant ideal; it is a quiet superpower available to you every single day.

Unmask Mental Health with Mind Power

If you are a parent, writer, educator or even a student - writing your new book or a board exam, don't worry but focus on what you can do. So, whether it is your academics or your professional life, let's see how this magic of Unmasking Holistic Mental Health can help us achieve excellence.

New Western Approach to Mental Health

Groundbreaking research from Stanford confirms that the mind actively rewires the body and brain in real time through our beliefs and thoughts. Neuroplasticity enables the brain to reshape itself by forming new neural connections based on repeated positive or negative inner dialogue.

Your mind is like a garden, your thoughts are the seeds. You can choose to plant flowers or weeds. Deeply held beliefs become reinforced neural pathways, but by challenging limiting thoughts, you can create new, healthier patterns.

Mental and emotional states influence the entire body via brain communication with bodily systems, including the immune system. Chronic stress and negative emotions release harmful hormones like cortisol, increasing inflammation and weakening health. Conversely, managing stress and fostering positive thoughts promote healing hormones that enhance natural recovery.

Mindfulness meditation has been scientifically shown to reduce inflammatory biomarkers like Interleukin-6 (IL-6) and improve stress resilience, supporting neuroplasticity and positive transformation in both brain and body.

Mental health challenges have two aspects:

- **Regular Care:** One essential aspect of addressing mental health challenges is the ongoing care and maintenance of both the body and the mind. This involves adopting positive practices and routines that support mental and physical well-being on a daily basis. Such regular attention helps to build resilience and prevent the onset of mental health difficulties.

- Curative Measures: The second aspect relates to the interventions and strategies required when an individual is experiencing mental health challenges. In these instances, specific actions and treatments are necessary to address and alleviate symptoms, helping the person recover and regain balance in their mental and emotional state.

Mental Health: Regular Care

Mindfulness improves mental health. In recent years, psychotherapists have turned to mindfulness meditation as an important element in the treatment of a number of problems, including - depression, substance abuse, eating disorders, couples' conflicts, anxiety disorders, and obsessive-compulsive disorder.

Professor emeritus Jon Kabat-Zinn, founder and former director of the Stress Reduction Clinic at the University of Massachusetts Medical Centre, helped to bring the practice of mindfulness meditation into mainstream medicine and demonstrated that practicing mindfulness can bring improvements in both physical and psychological symptoms as well as positive changes in health, attitudes, and behaviours.

Heal Your Mind to Heal Your Body

You hit the gym and workout regularly. As a health-freak you routinely consume fruits and vegetables. You get a good 7 to 8 hours of sleep each night. Despite all the care, your body develops bouts of illnesses, aches and pains. Do you have a burning question on your mind – *What more should I do to lead a healthy lifestyle?*

Acharya Satya Narayan Goenka, founder of Vipassana meditation movement in India, brought the practice of seeing things as they really are into mainstream. He says, *"Our thoughts and feelings create a subtle energy body. While diet and exercise influence physical health. A clean energy body is needed to sustain a perfect physical body. Any emotional blockages like fear, pain, confusion, anger or jealousy creates energy blockages in the energy body. It then manifests as an illness in our physical body."*

He adds, *"Let us cleanse our thoughts to radiate happiness and love to every cell of the body. Release past hurt to strengthen every organ. Forgive people to heal aches and pains. Remain calm and stable to cleanse the body. We have the power to create a healthy mind, which then creates a healthy body and a happy life."*

Remind yourself – *"My every thought creates happiness and health. All my health parameters are perfect. My body is healthy."*

Power of Your Thoughts

Also, if there is something troubling your body, do you know that you can use the power of your thoughts to influence your health? Each thought has an effect on the cells of our body. When we are physically unwell, we cure the body with medicines, but do we heal blockages in the mind? Just by thinking or saying – *My cholesterol is high… My fever isn't coming down, what will happen next… How will I manage to walk with this back pain…* we radiate an energy of sadness, worry or anxiety to our body. These vibrations slow down or block healing. Changing our thinking is as important as treating the body.

Brahma Kumari Sister Shivani's approach to mental health emphasises that thoughts create our reality and by mastering our inner world, we can overcome anxiety, stress, and depression. She teaches Rajyoga Meditation for the Brahma Kumaris, emphasising the power of thoughts and its higher connection for emotional independence and inner peace. Sister Shivani tells us:

Core Principles for Mental Well-Being

- **Thoughts create your reality:** Our thoughts are like seeds, and what we plant will shape our experiences. By consciously choosing positive, high-vibration thoughts, we can cultivate peace and joy.

- **Emotional independence:** True peace comes from within and is not dependent on external situations or people. Emotional independence means that your feelings are a product of your own thoughts, not other people's actions.

- **Peace is your original nature:** The peace is a natural, stable state of the soul that can be rediscovered through practices like meditation. By staying rooted in inner peace, you can navigate life's challenges with more grace and confidence.

- **The power of forgiveness:** Holding onto anger and resentment drains our mental energy. Forgiveness is a gift we give ourselves to find inner freedom, not a favour for the person who hurt us. It allows us to release emotional baggage and move forward.

- **Mindfulness:** It is crucial to be aware of your thoughts, not just your words and actions. By being mindful of the thoughts we create, we eliminate the need to control our words and behaviours.

Practical Techniques for Mental Wellbeing

- **Daily Affirmations:** Practice *Sankalp se siddhi* – 'what you resolve, you achieve' by setting clear intentions and repeating positive affirmations both in the morning and at night. For example, affirming "I am peaceful" or "I am powerful" helps reprogram the subconscious mind.

- **Meditation and Reflection:** Dedicate time each day for meditation to disconnect from the noise of the external world and reconnect with your peaceful inner self. Just a few minutes can help you stay calm and composed.

- **Emotional Diet:** Be conscious of the information you consume, and reduce exposure to work-related stress and social media, especially before bed. Spend 10 minutes journaling to process thoughts before you sleep.

- **Create "No-anger Zones":** In corporate or personal environments, consciously create «no-anger zones» to prevent stress from infecting the atmosphere. Encourage people to take time for themselves to prevent mental fatigue.

- **Take Time for Yourself:** Spend time alone to be with your own thoughts and prevent your mind from becoming reliant on external stimulants like gadgets. This helps you become more aware of your thought patterns and learn to be happy with yourself.

Mental Health: Curative Measures

Common Mental Health Challenges

Let us understand what challenges are faced by a person with disturbed mind. Some common mental health challenges are:

- **Stress:** Stress as an emotional disease is caused by uncomfortable emotions and unhealthy thought patterns. The solution is to create a peaceful inner state independent of external circumstances.

- **Depression and anxiety:** The root causes of these issues, such as negative thinking and social pressure. The spiritual practices can help heal the mind.

- **Overcoming fear and a disturbed mind:** Manage a disturbed mind by being aware of feelings like irritation and anxiety, which can manifest in your thoughts and body language. The guided meditations also focus on overcoming fear.

How caregivers can help

Caregivers profoundly influence mental health through the energy and vibrations their thoughts emit. Instead of focusing solely on the patient's behaviour, a caregiver's primary duty is to manage their own emotional and mental state effectively.

1. **Become Emotionally Independent:** Caregivers frequently take on others' negative emotions, which can sap their resilience. By focusing on your own well-being through practices like meditation, positive affirmations, and self-care, you can build inner strength. Emotional independence enables you to maintain calmness and conserve your energy.

2. **Radiate Positive Energy:** Thoughts are contagious. Your calm, positive mindset can create a supportive environment that encourages healing. Avoid pity or anxious worry, which produce negative energy. Instead, consciously generate thoughts of strength and recovery.

3. **Practice Unconditional Acceptance:** Trying to control others, breeds stress. Accept people as they are, recognising that healing begins with changing your own responses. Through patience and love, model emotional stability - a powerful lesson for those you support.

4. **Strengthen Your Mind Through Meditation:** Meditation builds resilience to emotional pressure. It aligns your energy with healing, supporting both yourself and the person in your care.

5. **Appreciate the Mind–Body Connection:** Your mindset plays a key role in recovery. Even with identical conditions, two people can have very different outcomes depending on their attitudes. Remember, lasting healing starts from within and should enhance, not replace, professional medical treatment.

Sometimes, the best medicine isn't a pill or a procedure - it's a shift in mindset. Let me share another story with you - a journey that takes us, without a passport, to London.

London Surgery Story (Dr Jackson)

Imagine a patient preparing for surgery. A couple of hours before the operation, a nurse fusses lovingly over the flowers in his hospital room.

She asks, "Sir, which surgeon is operating on you today?" The patient, half-drowsy, replies, "Dr Jackson." Suddenly, the nurse's face lights up.

"Dr Jackson? Are you sure? He's the busiest and most successful surgeon, with a 100% success rate! I can't believe he found time to operate on you. You're incredibly lucky!"

If you were in his place, wouldn't you feel as if you'd just won the lottery? The patient beams with gratitude, saying, "Yes, I am lucky. Thank you, God, and thank you, Dr Jackson."

As he's taken to surgery, buoyed by this confidence, the nurse continues to marvel, reinforcing his hope.

Here's the remarkable part: that nurse Susan, wasn't a nurse at all, but a psychologist trained in ancient Indian wisdom. Her role was to prepare the patient's mind long before the surgeon began his work.

She instilled confidence and hope - qualities that, according to both scientific research and storytelling, significantly contribute to healing. The surgery went well, and years later, the patient continues to be happy and healthy. During the pandemic, Susan happened to be my student and mentee. I first met her in 2018 when I was invited by the Hindu Society at King's College Hospital in London to deliver a keynote speech.

Reflections

So, what's the lesson here? Sometimes, the best medicine isn't a pill or procedure, it's a shift in mindset. Ancient Indian wisdom tells us: if you believe you can overcome your illness, you're already halfway there. This principle applies as much to mental health challenges like depression, stress, or relationship troubles, as it does to physical well-being.

With the right thoughts, a splash of humour, and a dash of ancient wisdom, even the toughest days can become stepping stones to growth. And if you ever falter - just recall Dr Jackson's story. Sometimes, all we need is a gentle reminder that the best hands looking after us… are our own.

Ingredients For Sound Mental Health

Regular Mindful Meditation

Regular mindful meditation is the soil in which several key mental-health qualities take root. Over time, it trains the mind to respond rather than react, and to stay steady even when life is not.

- **Respond, don't react:** Practise a brief pause before words or action so you can choose a wise response instead of an impulsive outburst.

- **Live objectively:** Stay informed and engaged but avoid getting emotionally entangled in every event; observe thoughts and feelings like passing clouds.

- **Maintain equanimity:** Reduce craving and aversion so you can move through highs and lows with a stable mind.

- **Deepen self-awareness:** Learn to see your own patterns clearly and adjust your behaviour; this is essential for success and healthy relationships.

- **Focus on strengths, not failures:** Build on your resilience, compassion, and skills instead of repeatedly replaying mistakes.

The path forward is consistent practice. Meditation, reflection, and honest self-observation gradually reduce mental agitation and purify the mind; progress shows up as greater balance, calmness, and clarity during everyday challenges.

Authenticity is another pillar of sound mental health. Many people wear social "masks" to please others, exhausting themselves in the process. True strength lies in gently dropping this conditioning and showing up as you are—supported by mindfulness, not performance.

The Law of Attraction adds an important layer: what you repeatedly think, speak, believe, and feel, you begin to manifest. Positive thinking, gratitude, and emotional regulation send out higher vibrations that support wellness, whereas chronic anxiety, bitterness, or self-pity lower your inner frequency and invite more distress.

As Sister Shivani advises, "Do not discuss endlessly the causes of failures, disappointments, setbacks, and environment." Keep your inner commentary enthusiastic, grateful, loving, relaxed, and appreciative.

Distinguishing Approaches for Mental Well-Being

A truly holistic approach recognises that *one size does not fit all* in mental health. Different levels of difficulty call for different types of support.

- **Complementary practices for everyday well-being:** For ordinary stress, worry, exam pressure, workload, or relationship friction, practices like mindfulness, affirmations, spiritual study, and the tools shared by teachers such as Sister Shivani are powerful. They build resilience, self-awareness, and a positive mindset, forming a strong base of mental well-being.

- **Medical intervention for severe illness:** For severe, chronic, or debilitating conditions - such as bipolar disorder, schizophrenia, or major depression, a combination of spiritual practice *and* professional medical care is often essential. These illnesses frequently involve neurobiological factors and require specialised treatment, including medication and structured therapy, under qualified professionals.

Honouring both paths is itself a sign of mental maturity. Using complementary practices for everyday balance while seeking medical help when illness is serious ensures that care is both compassionate and scientifically sound.

Mental Health and Indian Wisdom

Is Mental Health and Stress Related?

Let's get straight to a question I hear all the time: *"Captain, is mental health really connected to stress?"* Well, let me answer that with a little help from the Bhagavad Gita: My go-to guide for life's curveballs. In Chapter 6, verse 6, Lord Krishna says:

बन्धुरात्मात्मनस्तस्य येनात्मैवात्मना जितः |
अनात्मनस्तु शत्रुत्वे वर्ते तात्मैव शत्रुवत् || 6 ||

"For the one who has conquered the mind, the mind is the best of friends; but for one who has failed to do so, the mind will be the greatest enemy."

Key Points from Verse 6.6:

- **The Mind as a Friend:** If you have conquered your mind and senses, your own mind will act as your friend and best ally.

- **The Mind as an Enemy:** If you fail to conquer your mind, it becomes your greatest enemy, acting against you with its negative tendencies.

- **Conquest by Oneself:** The verse emphasises that conquering the mind is something that must be done "by oneself" through spiritual practice and self-discipline.

- **Internal Battle:** The verse highlights that the most significant «enemies» are not external but are the negative qualities residing within the mind, such as lust, anger, and attachment.

Emotions, my friends, are born in the mind. But let's not confuse emotions with pressure - they're cousins, not twins. Here's where science and math come to our rescue (don't worry, no exam at the end):

Stress, quite simply, is Pressure divided by Resilience. That's right,

Stress = Pressure ÷ Resilience

Wayne Dyer once said, *"The pressure has always been there."*

Tomorrow, it might be a new situation, but pressure is a lifelong companion. The trick is, stress isn't about the pressure itself - it's about our resilience, our ability to cope. Think about it: kids, athletes, soldiers on the front lines - they all face pressure, but what sets them apart is their training in resilience, their cool, positive mindset under fire.

So, what's the secret? Keep your resilience - the denominator - nice and high. If pressure goes up but resilience drops, stress shoots through the roof. That's when even a minor issue can feel like a full-blown crisis.

How to Take Care of Your Emotional Diet

Emotional resilience is not a quick fix; it is a daily discipline, just like physical fitness. To stay mentally strong, you need simple, repeatable habits that protect and train your mind over time.

A few decades ago, growing up meant no mobile phones, no internet, and hardly any television. Our "content diet" came mostly from parents, teachers, a few good books, and a single newspaper - our emotional world was smaller, and our elders acted as natural filters. Today, that gatekeeping has vanished, so you must consciously guard your emotional diet.

The way you feel is closely linked to the information you consume. Imagine your thoughts as mental nutrition: negative input leads to restless feelings. Begin by safeguarding the beginning and end of each day.

- **Morning:** Give the first hour to yourself - no phone, no news, no social media. Use this time for meditation, prayer, yoga, journaling, or uplifting reading. This is breakfast for your mind; do not start your day with emotional junk food.

- **Night:** The last hour before sleep sets the tone for your rest. Step away from screens and work-related stress at least 30 minutes before bed. Allow your mind to shift from high alert to gentle unwinding.

During the day, "charge" your mind as you would your phone. Practise brief pauses of mindfulness, observe your thoughts, and stop letting every person or situation hijack your inner state. Remember, the remote control of your feelings is in your hands, not in the hands of the world.

A simple formula captures this truth:

Stress = Pressure ÷ Resilience

You may not control the pressure, but you can strengthen the denominator - your resilience. When that denominator is strong, your mind becomes your greatest ally instead of your harshest critic.

Chapter Summary

Mental health, as explored in this chapter, is not a distant ideal but a daily discipline of **self-awareness, resilience, and authenticity**. From Stanford-backed neuroplasticity research showing how thoughts reshape the brain, to Sister Shivani's teachings on emotional independence, the message is clear: **the mind is both the sculptor and the sculpture**. Sound mental health grows through practices such as mindfulness, affirmations, a clean "emotional diet," and timely curative measures like meditation, therapy, and conscious self-reflection.

At its heart, this chapter invites you to live by a few simple principles:

- **Shake it off and step up:** Treat every challenge as a stepping stone, not a graveyard.

- **Mind over matter:** Your thoughts influence your chemistry, immunity, and healing.

- **Resilience multiplies calm:** Remember, **Stress = Pressure ÷ Resilience** - so keep your denominator strong.

- **Heal the mind to heal the body:** Emotional cleanliness supports physical wellbeing.

- **Practise emotional independence:** True peace is generated within, not outsourced to people or circumstances.

- **Mind your diet:** Guard the mental and emotional inputs you allow into your inner world.

- **Be authentic:** Drop the masks; strength lies in being inwardly aligned, not outwardly perfect.

- **Law of Attraction:** What you repeatedly focus on expands in your inner and outer life.

Reflect & Apply

Use these prompts to move from insight to integration:

- Identify one limiting belief you have carried for years. How can you reframe it using the lens of neuroplasticity and new thought patterns?

- What does **emotional independence** mean to you at home or at work? Where are you still handing others the "remote control" of your feelings?

- How will you strengthen your **resilience denominator** this week – through meditation, journaling, exercise, therapy, or positive input?

- Review your **mental diet.** Which media, conversations, or habits can you reduce or replace to protect your peace of mind?

- In which areas of life can you better align thoughts, emotions, and actions to live more authentically, without masks or pretence?

Mental health, ultimately, is being your authentic self – confident, calm, and self-trusting, without hiding behind fear, roles, or expectations.

APPENDIX 1

Breath Awareness & Self Focusing Meditation

*~ A foundational set of practices to cultivate calm, focus,
and heightened self-awareness.*

The Nature of Meditation

Meditation is a skill, one that, like any other, improves with consistent practice. Mastery comes through repetition. The more often you meditate, the better you understand its workings and the richer your experience becomes.

Yet for many, meditation can feel dry or mechanical when there is no sense of peace, harmony, or stillness arising from within. This is why genuine experience is so important. Only when we tangibly feel the shifts - greater poise amidst chaos, a deeper sense of calm, do we feel inspired to continue. This appendix guides you through practical, step-by-step instructions for mindful meditations designed to cultivate this inner experience.

Guided Meditation – Mindful Breath Awareness (MBA)

(For detailed instructions, see Chapter 3)

The secret is in consistent practice. Most find that about 20 - 30 minutes is ideal.

Let's begin…

Begin by gently resting your attention at the entrance of your nostrils. This is where you will first begin to notice sensations: perhaps warmth, coolness, tingling, subtle throbbing, or gentle vibrations. Each sensation is a sign that your awareness is becoming more refined.

Let this practice become your anchor to mindfulness and presence, available whenever you seek balance, clarity, or a moment of deep calm.

Let's begin by gently closing your eyes. Allow yourself to settle into a comfortable position. Notice your body starting to relax and your breath moving naturally. Soften your face and hands. Just breathe comfortably.

Make a Resolution

Quietly, within, repeat this intention three times:
"I am practising breath awareness for the purification of my mind."

Stage One: Arrive in the Moment

Turn your attention to the present. Notice the sounds around you, the sensations in your body, and any thoughts or feelings that arise. Simply observe them, do not follow or engage with them. Continue breathing softly, aware and relaxed, fully here and now.

Stage Two: Body Awareness

Become gently aware of your whole body. Notice how your body feels - any places of comfort or discomfort, the support beneath you, the gentle movement of breathing. If you find any physical tension, allow it to melt away on the next out-breath. If there is worry or anxiety, permit it to rest. With each breath, invite ease into mind and body.

Stage Three: Awareness of Breath

Now, notice the breath as it moves through your body. As you inhale, feel the stomach gently expand; as you exhale, feel it release. Observe the breath flowing through your nose, chest, and abdomen. There's no need to hurry - just breathe easily, witnessing each breath.

Stage Four: Focusing at the Nostrils

Gently bring your attention to the tip of your nose. Notice air moving in and out of the nostrils - how it feels as you breathe in, how it feels as you breathe out. Let all your attention rest at the nostrils, simply observing the natural flow of breath, without effort. Breathing happens by itself.

(Continue for 15 minutes with intermittent reminders...)

Whenever thoughts, sounds, or images arise, just return to the breath. If you wish, begin counting each exhale from one to ten to stay centred.

If your attention drifts away, you may slightly deepen or quicken your breath for a few rounds to refresh awareness, then settle back into your natural rhythm.

After 15 Minutes

Become aware of a deep stillness, the vastness of the sky, the brilliance of light from above, and your presence – stable, calm, and centred.

Repeat to yourself:

- *"I shall do the right thing – I shall respond thoughtfully, not react impulsively."*

- *"I will not criticise myself or dwell in guilt."*

- *"I will set my emotions aside and bring kindness into my thoughts, words, and actions."*

Hold the intention to radiate loving-kindness and non-injury, wishing well for all.

Affirmation and Visualisation

Picture a golden shower of light streaming gently from your head to your toes, filling you with healing energy. Feel this light nourishing every part of your body and mind.

Forgiveness

- *Silently forgive all who have hurt you, knowingly or unknowingly, and release them gently from your life.*

- *Invite forgiveness from all whom you may have hurt, knowingly or unknowingly.*

- *Forgiveness is much more than letting go; it is an act of love for the soul. It does not erase the past but allows us to view it with compassion and mercy. Forgiveness liberates your soul and dissolves fear.*

- *It is not just pardoning others but nurturing your own emotional wellbeing, a beautiful and permanent transformation, an acceptance of your inner power and unconditional love.*

- *Release your ego. Release your past. Seek forgiveness with complete faith and belief.*

Gratitude

- *Offer gratitude now: Thank you, Universe, God, Guru, Guides, Family, and Self for blessing me with a good heart, clear mind, strong hands, agile body, and steady legs. Thank you for nourishing food, clean air to breathe, and bountiful nature that supports my growth.*

- *Raise your right hand to your chest, palm facing outward.*

- *Visualise golden light flowing from your palm to Mother Earth. Bless the Earth with joy, healing, kindness, beauty, and peace. Bless all people with love and bliss.*

- *Say silently, "Thank you, thank you, thank you," for these priceless blessings.*

Closing Affirmations and Awakening

- *Visualise your smiling face radiating with positive energy. Repeat silently three times,*
  "I am a peaceful soul. I am a powerful soul. I am a lovable soul."

- *When ready, I will count from one to three, and you will slowly open your eyes feeling refreshed, alert, and healthier than before.*

- *One… two… coming back slowly… three… eyes open, wide awake, feeling wonderful. Better than before. Do not open your eyes abruptly. Gently look down at your lap. Then slowly look up.*

Integration and Reflection

Remember: Practice daily, morning and evening, to deepen your connection with this powerful meditation tool. You now possess a technique to use your mind intentionally - for healing, intuition, and vividly creating your future.

One reality you may begin to notice is the mind's habit of constantly wandering to the past or the future. This is natural. With breath awareness, you gently retrain the mind to stay in the present. Each time you bring it back, you strengthen your ability to live moment to moment, the only place where true peace is found.

Enhance Your Visualisation

(For detailed instructions, see Chapter 4)

Our goal here is to sharpen your sensory faculties through vivid and multi-sensory visualisation.

- *Sit comfortably and softly close your eyes.*

- **Visualise:** *Begin to visualise a range of colours - red, blue, green and notice their shades and intensities. Picture shapes, from round to flat, intricate to simple.*

- **Sound:** *Now bring in sounds - feel the gentle hum of the wind, distant traffic, the buzz of an aeroplane overhead, the honk of a car horn, the chime of a doorbell or phone. Hear the roar of vehicles, the rustle of dry leaves, voices calling names from afar to nearby.*

- **Touch:** *Touch the textures within your mind's eye. Experience the temperature, the feel of smoothness or roughness, wetness or dryness. Imagine touching ripe fruit, soft leaves, a pillow you squeeze, a sponge, or the skin of a loved one. Recall the first thing you touched this morning and feel it vividly.*

- **Taste:** *Turn to taste. Recall flavours of salt, sugar, honey, tangy lemon, tea, and rich coffee. Taste them fully in your imagination.*

- *Then breathe life into a simple image: three apples resting in your hand - red, green, and yellow. Experience their colour, texture, weight, taste, and even the soft sound as you handle them.*

- *When ready, open your eyes.*

Reflect on the Experience: Did you enjoy this exercise? Notice that you are experiencing these sensations as if they have already happened, programming your mind toward that future reality with sensory richness.

Alternate Visualisation Exercise

- *Sit in a comfortable posture and gently close your eyes.*

- *Use deep breathing - take three slow, full breaths, to enter your Ideal State.*

- *From this relaxed state, mentally transport yourself to any room in your home, perhaps your kitchen or living room and imagine you are fully present in that space.*

- *Using the power of memory, explore the room around you: notice what lies before you, behind you, to your left, and to your right.*

- *Focus your attention on a single wall. Observe every detail: the colour, wallpaper patterns, pictures, windows, curtains, light switches, clocks, furniture, and appliances. Notice the colours and textures with clarity.*
- *Ask yourself:*
  - *What am I seeing in my mind's eye right now?*
  - *What images arise when I think about the world around me, or the people in my life?*
  - *What visions come to mind when I think about my future - positive or negative, fuzzy or crystal clear?*
- *The clearest images in your mind are those you are most likely to experience.*
- *When ready, open your eyes.*

With consistent application of mindful and visualisation techniques, you can reshape the images you hold about the world and your role in it, gradually transforming your experiences and outcomes.

Guided Meditation – Mindful Self-Focusing: 3-2-1

(For detailed instructions, see Chapter 4)

Let's begin…

Find a comfortable sitting position. Back straight but relaxed. Follow the instructions. If you miss anything, it's OK. Smile on your face. Adjust your body now. Keep your body still. Gently close your eyes.

Make a Resolution

Quietly, within, repeat this intention three times:
"I am practising mindful meditation for the purification of my mind."

If your mind is agitated, practice breath awareness for 5 to 10 minutes. Then begin 3-2-1 self-focusing mindful meditation.

Level Three: Physical Relaxation

This level helps you deeply relax your body, from head to toe, in moments. To guide you, I'll lead your attention through each part of your body:

Take a deep breath. As you exhale, mentally repeat and visualise the number THREE, three times.

First, awareness of head, face and throat.

- *Bring your awareness to the top of your head, the scalp and skin. You may notice a fine vibration, warmth from circulation, or tingling. Now, release any tension or tightness here. Sink into a state of growing, deep relaxation.*

- *Shift your focus to your forehead. Again, sense gentle vibrations and warmth, then release tension completely. Let relaxation deepen with each breath.*

- *Now, bring awareness to your face – the skin around your eyes, cheeks, nose, lips, ears, and chin. Feel subtle sensations and warmth. Release all tension here and sink deeper into relaxation.*

- *Focus on your throat. Notice the skin, the internal parts such as your windpipe, and the subtle sensations. Relax all muscles, ligaments, and tissues here – deepen the calm.*

- *Move to your shoulders and arms. Feel your clothes against your skin; notice sensations along your shoulders, upper arms, elbows, forearms, wrists, fingers, and palms. Let go of all tension and let this area relax deeply and completely.*

Next, your chest. *Feel the breath moving naturally in your lungs and heart area. Sense the warmth of your skin covering your chest. Relax all tissues, cells, glands, and organs to beat and function rhythmically in health. Allow this relaxed state to deepen.*

Now, your abdomen. *Feel your clothing and skin on your belly, including organs like liver, spleen, intestines, kidneys, and reproductive organs. Let every tissue, cell, gland, and organ relax and work in harmony. Allow this deep relaxation to grow stronger.*

Move to your thighs. *Notice sensations and pressures on your thighs. Feel the bones and muscles subtly vibrating. Release all tension here and allow deep relaxation to envelop this area.*

Knees and calves. *Bring awareness to these joints and muscles. Feel your skin's sensations, then soften and relax completely with every breath.*

Feet, ankles, heels, soles, and toes. *Be aware of the skin and sensations here. Let go of tension and feel profound relaxation spreading through your feet and lower legs.*

Visualising the Body from Outside. *Imagine your feet, ankles, calves, knees, thighs, waist, shoulders, arms, and hands as separate from you – as if you are witnessing your body from the outside, as a soul or self.*

Entering a Deep, Healthy Mind State. *You are now at a deeper, healthier level of mind, deeper than before. This is your level three physical relaxation. Whenever you mentally repeat and visualise the number THREE, your body will relax to this deep, refreshing state and even deeper with continued practice. When ready, bring attention back to your body and feel the support of your chair. Keep your eyes closed, remain still, and carry a gentle smile.*

Level TWO – Mental Relaxation

Take a slow, deep breath, and as you exhale, mentally repeat and visualise the number TWO, three times.

Level Two is all about mental relaxation. Even if you hear noises around you, instead of distracting you, they become part of your calming practice, helping your mind relax more deeply. Mental relaxation means your thoughts are peaceful and calm, focused on pleasant and positive surroundings.

To guide you, I will take you through several serene, joyful scenes. As you visualise these, you allow your mind to settle and your stress to ease.

Imagine yourself:

- *On a warm beach under the sun, feeling the sand beneath you and hearing soft waves.*

- *Gently boating on a still, mirror-like lake surrounded by nature's quiet beauty.*

- *Sitting in a humble thatched hut beside a peaceful riverbank, sharing wisdom with your mentor.*

- *Walking through a lush forest on a perfect summer day, feeling the gentle breeze, surrounded by tall trees, blooming flowers, birds singing softly, and squirrels darting playfully.*

You are now resting in a deeper, healthier state of mind – mental relaxation Level Two. With each practice, your body relaxes more fully whenever you bring your awareness to the number TWO.

Keep practising by visualising other happy scenes: drifting clouds, flowing rivers, calming beaches, or majestic mountains. These images will nourish your mental calm.

Level ONE – Basic Level of Relaxation

Take a slow, deep breath. As you exhale, mentally repeat and visualise the number ONE, three times.

You are now entering Level One – a basic yet powerful state of relaxation that serves as the gateway to deeper, healthier levels of mind.

To help you go deeper, I will count down slowly from 10 to 1. With every descending number, allow yourself to relax more profoundly, sinking gently into a calm, clear, and healthy state of mind.

- *10… 9… feel yourself going deeper.*

- *8… 7… 6… descending further and deeper.*

- *5… 4… 3… relaxing more and more.*

- *2… 1… now fully settled into a deeper, healthier state of mind.*

At this level, you have complete control over your senses and faculties, including your waking conscious mind. Feel this soothing relaxation flow slowly throughout your entire body – down your neck, arms, torso, legs, all the way to your toes.

It's a wonderful feeling, being deeply relaxed and fully centred in a rejuvenating state of health.

To guide you even further, I will count from one to three and snap my fingers. As you hear the snap, project your mind to your ideal place of relaxation, a place where you feel completely at ease.

I will pause speaking now, and when you next hear my voice, one hour will have passed in this restful state, yet you will feel alert and refreshed, without surprise.

Take a deep breath. As you exhale, relax more deeply. Whenever you hear the word "relax," all unnecessary movements and mental activity cease. You are completely relaxed physically and mentally…

One… Two… Three… snap!

Relax… relax… relax…

When ready, begin to return gently.

The difference between a genius mindset and ordinary thinking is that geniuses access and use more of their mind, especially the intuitive and creative parts. You are now learning to tap into this greater potential in a special way.

Repeat mentally after me:

- *"My mental faculties grow stronger every day, serving humanity better and better."*

- *"Each day, in every way, I improve more and more."*

- *"Positive thoughts bring me the benefits and opportunities I desire."*

You have full mastery over your sensing faculties at all levels of mind, including your conscious waking state.

Use this mental training to help yourself, your loved ones, or anyone in need of physical or mental support. Always direct this power constructively, creatively, and with pure intentions – for goodness, honesty, and positivity.

This practice is your contribution to leaving a better world for those who follow.

Think of all humanity as your family – mothers, fathers, brothers, sisters, sons, and daughters. You are a compassionate, understanding, and patient human being, growing in true greatness.

Forgiveness

Silently forgive all who have hurt you, knowingly or unknowingly, and release them gently from your life.

Invite forgiveness from all whom you may have hurt.

Forgiveness is much more than letting go; it is an act of love for the soul. It does not erase the past but allows us to view it with compassion and mercy. Forgiveness liberates your soul and dissolves fear.

It is not just pardoning others but nurturing your own emotional wellbeing, a beautiful and permanent transformation, an acceptance of your inner power and unconditional love.

Release your ego. Release your past. Seek forgiveness with complete faith and belief.

Gratitude

Offer gratitude now: Thank you, Universe, God, Guru, Guides, Family, and Self for blessing me with a good heart, clear mind, strong hands, agile body, and steady legs. Thank you for nourishing food, clean air to breathe, and bountiful nature that supports my growth.

Raise your right hand to your chest, palm facing outward.

Visualise golden light flowing from your palm to Mother Earth. Bless the Earth with joy, healing, kindness, beauty, and peace. Bless all people with love and bliss.

Say silently, "Thank you, thank you, thank you," for these priceless blessings.

Closing Affirmations and Awakening

Visualise your smiling face radiating with positive energy. Repeat silently three times,
"I am a peaceful soul. I am a powerful soul. I am a lovable soul."

When ready, I will count from one to three, and you will slowly open your eyes feeling refreshed, alert, and healthier than before.

One… two… coming back slowly… three… eyes open, wide awake, feeling wonderful. Better than before. Do not open your eyes abruptly. Gently look down at your lap. Then slowly look up.

Reflections

I hope you enjoyed this practice. Self-Focusing Mindful Meditation using the 3-2-1 method has been close to my heart since I began at fifteen. It has deeply transformed my life and continues to support hundreds of practitioners in cultivating peace, happiness, and spiritual wellbeing.

You have just learned a powerful mental tool that you will revisit frequently to build intuition, purify your mind, and visualise your magnificent future.

APPENDIX 2

VAK Sensory Meditation

*~ Training Your Visual, Auditory,
and Kinaesthetic Mind to Heal and Grow.*

Demystifying the Spiritual Path

Rooted in ancient Indian wisdom and refined over thousands of years, these meditations - including Yog Nidra, Vipassana, and Preksha Dhyan, tap into the mind's powerful creative potential. Paramhansa Yogananda once said, "Our consciousness creates our world, and with proper training, you can learn to shift your mind."

Key Tips for Effective Practice

- Notice sensations deeply, observing their fleeting nature to help transform old patterns of thought and behaviour.

- Follow guided visualisation and positive affirmations attentively. If you lose track, don't worry - gently return to awareness of the present moment.

- Engage all five senses in your visualisations to make them vivid and real—feel the breeze, smell fragrances, and sense the textures around you.

This foundational work of visualisation (see Appendix 1) and mindfulness meditation equips you to consciously and creatively harness the power of your mind, supporting profound personal transformation and successful goal attainment.

Let us journey together to understand the spiritual dimension of meditation - not through hearsay, faith, or beliefs, but through direct experience. By meditating and observing what arises, you gain insights grounded in your own mindful practice.

Meditation Exercise for VAK – Positive / Pleasant Images

(For detailed instructions, see Chapter 9)

Gently close your eyes and relax. Keep your eyes closed throughout this exercise. Bring your attention softly to your breath, feeling its natural rhythm.

Now, recall a delightful memory, something joyful and uplifting. It may be recent or from long ago. Allow this memory to come vividly to mind.

Imagine this memory becoming brighter and more radiant. As you enhance its brightness, observe how your mood shifts, becoming lighter and happier.

Next, bring this mental image closer to you, as if it is right in front of you. Then, make the image larger – see it grow in size and detail.

Notice how changing the image's size and proximity affects your experience. The feelings become more intense; the experience becomes more vivid and joyous.

For most, making a positive memory bigger, closer, and brighter enhances the experience, intensifying internal representation and bringing a deeper sense of happiness.

Let's explore another sensory dimension – sound.

Recall the same pleasant memory. Imagine the sounds associated with it becoming louder and richer. Add rhythm, deepen the bass, and imagine changes in tone and clarity. Make the sounds more vivid and joyful.

Now, bring your awareness to touch and movement – the kinaesthetic sense.

Feel the memory becoming warmer, softer, and smoother. Sense the textures, weight, and temperature of everything connected to that memory.

When you are ready, gently open your eyes.

Reflection

Notice how your feelings have shifted. Everyone responds differently, especially to kinesthetics sensations. Many people find that increasing brightness and size of the image intensifies positive emotions, placing them in a more resourceful and joyful state.

You might notice physical signs too – deeper breathing, straighter posture, a relaxed face, and an overall alert, calm presence.

Now, apply this same practice to negative or unpleasant images.

Meditation Exercise for VAK – Negative / Unpleasant Images

(For detailed instructions, see Chapter 9)

Gently close your eyes and relax. Keep your eyes closed throughout the practice, focusing on your breath.

Bring to mind an upsetting or painful image. Notice how it makes you feel.

Begin by making this negative image brighter, larger, and closer. What happens? Most people find the discomfort or pain intensifies along with the image.

Now, slowly move the image back to where it was. Make it smaller, dimmer, and further away.

Notice the difference in your emotional state. Often, the negative emotions decrease, becoming less overwhelming.

Repeat this process mindfully and intensely. Notice which sensory modalities— visual, auditory, kinaesthetic—have the greatest impact on you.

Explore the negative image again:

- *Make it smaller, softer, fuzzier, and dimmer - harder to see clearly.*

- *Mentally push it away, imagining it dissolving into a distant sun.*

- *Observe what you hear, see, and feel as the image fades away.*

Do the same with sounds related to the negative image:

- *Quiet the volume of any voices.*

- *Make them slower, less rhythmic, and less sharp.*

Finally, address kinesthetics sensations:

- *Imagine the negative feelings becoming dry, weak, drooping, and unimportant—like a fragile straw.*

When ready, gently open your eyes.

Reflection

You'll likely find the negative image has lost its power - becoming less painful, sometimes disappearing entirely. This practice allows you to gradually dissolve old hurts, freeing space for peace and strength.

You have two choices in life: Let your mind wander in habitual patterns, or choose consciously to guide it, planting seeds of joy, passion, and vitality.

This exercise offers a powerful pathway to enriching your internal world and creating a more vibrant life.

Whoosh Pattern

(For detailed instructions, see Chapter 9)

Step # 1: Identify the behaviour you want to change. For example, if you're going to stop biting your fingernails, imagine a picture of yourself lifting your hand, bringing your fingers to your lips, and biting your nails.

Step # 2: Create a different representation of the desired change. You might picture yourself taking your fingers away from your mouth, creating a little pressure on the finger you would bite, and seeing your nails perfectly manicured and yourself magnificently groomed. This picture should be disassociated.

Step # 3: "Whoosh" the two pictures so the un-resourceful experience automatically triggers the resourceful experience.

Process 1: *Gently close your eyes …*

- *Start by creating a bright picture of the behaviour you want to change.*

- *Then, in the bottom right-hand corner of that picture, make a small dark picture of how you want to be.*

- *Take that tiny picture, and in less than a second, have it grown in size and brightness and burst through the picture of the behaviour you no longer desire.*

- *As you do this process, say "whoosh" with all the enthusiasm and excitement you can.*

- *Open your eyes for a split second to break the state.*

- *Close your eyes again to do the swish once more.*

- *Pause and experience it. Open your eyes. Close your eyes. See what you want to change. Whoosh it again.*

- *Do this five or six times as fast as you can.*

Process 2: *Gently close your eyes …*

- *Imagine a slingshot in front of you.*

- *Between the two posts is a picture of the present behaviour you want to change.*

- *Place a small picture of how you want to be in the sling.*

- *Then, mentally watch this little picture being pulled farther back until the sling is stretched as far as possible.*

- *Then let it go. Watch as it explodes through the old picture before you and into your brain.*

- *It is essential that when you do this, you mentally pull the sling back before letting it go.*

- *You still say "whoosh" as you release it and break through the old limiting picture of yourself.*

- *When you let go of the sling, the picture should come at you so fast that your head snaps back.*

- *Pause and take a moment to think of some limiting thoughts you would like to change.*

- *Do this five or six times as fast as you can.*

The key to this process is speed and having fun doing it. You are telling your mind: see this, whoosh, do this, see this, whoosh, do this, see this … until the old picture automatically triggers the new picture and thus the new behaviour.

Meditation is for Upbringing and Self Discovery

Buddha was asked, "What have you gained from meditation?"

"Nothing," Buddha replied. "However, let me tell you what I lost - anger, Anxiety, Depression, Insecurity, Fear of old age and death.

Meditation is thus a profound practice for self-upbringing, self-discovery, and ultimately, self-enlightenment.

A mind that is quiet and subdued becomes truly ready for meditation. The final three verses of Chapter 5 of the Bhagavad Gita offer guidance on the practice of meditation and the path to self-realisation.

We seek to experience the benefits of meditation here and now - not a week or month later, but instantly. Therefore, we commit to meditating regularly and openly, ready to feel the promise of transformation in the present moment.

Let us approach meditation with the mindset of a scientist: setting up an experiment, observing outcomes, and arriving at conclusions based on direct experience. In this way, we bring scientific rigor to the field of spirituality.

Common Affirmations to Be Part of Every Meditation Session

Affirmation and Visualisation

Picture a golden shower of light streaming gently from your head to your toes, filling you with healing energy. Feel this light nourishing every part of your body and mind.

Forgiveness

- *Silently forgive all who have hurt you, knowingly or unknowingly, and release them gently from your life.*

- *Invite forgiveness from all whom you may have hurt, knowingly or unknowingly.*

- *Forgiveness is much more than letting go; it is an act of love for the soul. It does not erase the past but allows us to view it with compassion and mercy. Forgiveness liberates your soul and dissolves fear.*

- *It is not just pardoning others but nurturing your own emotional wellbeing, a beautiful and permanent transformation, an acceptance of your inner power and unconditional love.*

- *Release your ego. Release your past. Seek forgiveness with complete faith and belief.*

Gratitude

- *Offer gratitude now: Thank you, Universe, God, Guru, Guides, Family, and Self for blessing me with a good heart, clear mind, strong hands, agile body, and steady legs. Thank you for nourishing food, clean air to breathe, and bountiful nature that supports my growth.*

- *Raise your right hand to your chest, palm facing outward.*

- *Visualise golden light flowing from your palm to Mother Earth. Bless the Earth with joy, healing, kindness, beauty, and peace. Bless all people with love and bliss.*

- *Say silently, "Thank you, thank you, thank you," for these priceless blessings.*

Closing Affirmations and Awakening

- *Visualise your smiling face radiating with positive energy. Repeat silently three times,*
  "I am a peaceful soul. I am a powerful soul. I am a lovable soul."

- *When ready, I will count from one to three, and you will slowly open your eyes feeling refreshed, alert, and healthier than before.*

- *One… two… coming back slowly… three… eyes open, wide awake, feeling wonderful. Better than before. Do not open your eyes abruptly. Gently look down at your lap. Then slowly look up.*

Goal Setting & Spiritual Guides

*~ Techniques to engage your inner wisdom
and intuition via creative mental imagery.*

Welcome to the Visualisation Zone - a powerful space where your inner resources and spiritual guides come alive to assist your journey. With a clear purpose and a solid plan, you can maintain motivation and momentum through every challenge. Now, let's explore how to focus your mind to receive guidance, inspiration, and clarity in your quest.

This programme will guide you through my proven, practical process for achieving any goal, no matter how big. First, you learn to define your extraordinary life - your true purpose. Then, you select a goal that aligns with this highest vision and start clearing any obstacles that might be holding you back, accelerating your path toward success.

To fulfil your purpose, you may have several smaller goals. Each goal completed is a victory on your path. Here, you will learn mindful techniques to programme your mind and steadily achieve these goals by mirroring your thoughts and intentions.

Mirror the Mind: Mehtod - 1

Prepare to commence meditation:

- Select your goal and prepare to begin.

- Anchor your three fingers gently (see previous exercises/Appendix 2).

- Take a deep belly breath, and relax your body from head to toe, releasing tension.

Guided Meditation for Mirror the Mind: Method – 1

(For detailed instructions, see Chapter 11)

Let's begin…

Find a comfortable sitting position. Back straight but relaxed. Follow the instructions. If you miss anything, it's OK. Smile on your face. Adjust your body now. Keep your body still. Gently close your eyes.

Make a Resolution

- *Keep breathing slowly and rhythmically, repeating your intention mentally two or three times: "I am relaxing deeply as I mirror my mind."*

- *If your mind is agitated, practice breath awareness for 5 to 10 minutes.*

- *Imagine a large mental screen, like a giant TV, positioned about six to ten feet in front of you and slightly above your horizon line.*

- *Tilt your eyes upward about 20 degrees with eyes closed. This stimulates alpha brainwave activity, helping you relax deeply and connect with your inner mind.*

Descend Into Deep Relaxation

- *I will count from ten to one, with each descending number, you will go deeper into relaxation:*

- *10… 9… feel yourself unwinding.*
  8… 7… 6… deeper, calmer.
  5… 4… 3… more serene.
  2… 1… entering your deepest, healthiest mental state.

- *When in this peaceful state with your fingers anchored, mentally affirm: "This is my state of total relaxation for mirroring my mind."*

- *Unlock your fingers gently.*

Working with the Mental Screen

- *Visualise the screen you imagined earlier. On it, project an image of your current situation – place it inside a frame - coloured blue, reflecting your present challenges.*

- *Study this image calmly and let it fade away, erased by your hand.*

- *Hold the frame by both hands. Move this frame to one side and change its colour to white.*

- *Now project an outcome image inside the white frame – a bright, detailed, and compelling picture of your desired achievement.*

Embodying Your Future Self

- *Allow this new image to grow, bring it closer, and eventually step into this vision. Become one with the successful, accomplished you.*

- *Feel the joy of thriving and flourishing exactly as you want.*

- *Seal the state by pressing your three fingers together.*
  Mentally say: "When I press my fingers, I access this powerful, resourceful self."

- *Use this anchor anytime you need confidence, strength, or focus.*

Forgiveness

- *Silently forgive all who have hurt you, knowingly or unknowingly, and release them gently from your life.*

- *Invite forgiveness from all whom you may have hurt.*

- *Forgiveness is much more than letting go; it is an act of love for the soul. It does not erase the past but allows us to view it with compassion and mercy. Forgiveness liberates your soul and dissolves fear.*

- *It is not just pardoning others but nurturing your own emotional wellbeing, a beautiful and permanent transformation, an acceptance of your inner power and unconditional love.*

- *Release your ego. Release your past. Seek forgiveness with complete faith and belief.*

Gratitude

- *Offer gratitude now: Thank you, Universe, God, Guru, Guides, Family, and Self for blessing me with a good heart, clear mind, strong hands, agile body, and steady legs. Thank you for nourishing food, clean air to breathe, and bountiful nature that supports my growth.*

- *Raise your right hand to your chest, palm facing outward.*

- *Visualise golden light flowing from your palm to Mother Earth. Bless the Earth with joy, healing, kindness, beauty, and peace. Bless all people with love and bliss.*

- *Say silently, "Thank you, thank you, thank you," for these priceless blessings.*

Closing Affirmations and Awakening

- *Visualise your smiling face radiating with positive energy. Repeat silently three times,*
  "I am a peaceful soul. I am a powerful soul. I am a lovable soul."

- *When ready, I will count from one to three, and you will slowly open your eyes feeling refreshed, alert, and healthier than before.*

- *One… two… coming back slowly… three… eyes open, wide awake, feeling wonderful. Better than before. Do not open your eyes abruptly. Gently look down at your lap. Then slowly look up.*

Practice, practice – in the morning when you wake up and before going to sleep at night.

This Mirror of the Mind technique is a potent tool for transforming your mindset and realising your highest aims. Practice it regularly to deepen your connection with your inner guidance and manifest your desired future.

Mirror the Mind: Method – 2

When you programme your mind at the Alpha state, the subconscious level - your faith, intense desire, belief, expectancy, and repetition (DBER) empower you to manifest your goals. Throughout your day, you can activate this power by using a simple physical cue: your three-finger anchor.

At any moment when you wish to recall a positive state or strengthen your connection to your goal, gently press your three fingers together, close your eyes briefly, and invoke the feeling associated with your intention. This anchor keeps you aligned with your purpose and motivates you toward success, joy, and fulfilment in the coming year and beyond.

Creating Your Vision and Programme

Choose a goal that resonates deeply with you. For example, optimum health.

Visualise an outcome image of having achieved this goal - vivid, detailed, and emotionally charged.

Reflect on how strongly you believe in this vision and the energy of your belief. Be congruent: let your thoughts, intentions, and actions walk the same path. Clarify your purpose - perhaps health, service to others, or financial wellbeing—and commit to it.

Guided Meditation for Mirror the Mind: Method - 2

(For detailed instructions, see Chapter 11)

Prepare to commence meditation:

- Select your goal and prepare to begin.

- Anchor your three fingers gently (see previous exercises/Appendix 2).

- Take a deep belly breath, and relax your body from head to toe, releasing tension.

Let's begin...

Find a comfortable sitting position. Back straight but relaxed. Follow the instructions. If you miss anything, it's OK. Smile on your face. Adjust your body now. Keep your body still. Gently close your eyes.

Make a Resolution

Keep breathing slowly and rhythmically, repeating your intention mentally two or three times: "I am relaxing deeply as I mirror my mind."

If your mind is agitated, practice breath awareness for 5 to 10 minutes.

Imagine a giant mental screen, like a large TV, placed about six to ten feet in front of you and slightly above eye level.

Visualising Your Goal

Focus on your chosen goal on the mental screen. If you're new to this, imagine your goal unfolding over the next three years. Ask yourself:

- *What does your optimum health look like?*

- *How does it feel in your body and mind?*

- *Who shares this success journey with you—family, friends, colleagues?*

- *Spend a minute fully immersed in this vision.*

Anchoring and Deepening

- *Recall the number three, slowly repeating it three times, feeling your body relax profoundly.*

- *Repeat the number two three times, immersing in deep mental relaxation.*

- *Then repeat the number one three times, entering the Alpha state—a serene, focused mental level.*

- *Now see your mental screen filling your vision - a vivid theatre of your future health from …... (say January) onward.*

- *Radiate healing energy through affirmations such as:*

  - *"All is perfect."*

  - *"My body is relaxed and healing."*

  - *"I accept my body, and it accepts me."*

  - *"I create harmony and health through my mind."*

Enhancing the Vision

- *Add colour, sound, and sensations to your mental image. Engage your senses fully - see the vibrancy, feel the wellness, experience the joy.*

- *If colours or details seem faint, practice image streaming: describe aloud or mentally every aspect you perceive. Speaking your observations sharpens and enriches the image, making it more vivid.*

- *Repeat affirmations such as – "I am perfectly healthy. Every cell relaxes and functions optimally. My body responds well to treatment. I am healed and strong."*

Forgiveness

- *Silently forgive all who have hurt you, knowingly or unknowingly, and release them gently from your life.*

- *Invite forgiveness from all whom you may have hurt, knowingly or unknowingly.*

- *Forgiveness is much more than letting go; it is an act of love for the soul. It does not erase the past but allows us to view it with compassion and mercy. Forgiveness liberates your soul and dissolves fear.*

- *It is not just pardoning others but nurturing your own emotional wellbeing, a beautiful and permanent transformation, an acceptance of your inner power and unconditional love.*

- *Release your ego. Release your past. Seek forgiveness with complete faith and belief.*

Gratitude

- *Offer gratitude now: Thank you, Universe, God, Guru, Guides, Family, and Self for blessing me with a good heart, clear mind, strong hands, agile body, and steady legs. Thank you for nourishing food, clean air to breathe, and bountiful nature that supports my growth.*

- *Raise your right hand to your chest, palm facing outward.*

- *Visualise golden light flowing from your palm to Mother Earth. Bless the Earth with joy, healing, kindness, beauty, and peace. Bless all people with love and bliss.*

- *Say silently, "Thank you, thank you, thank you," for these priceless blessings.*

Closing Affirmations and Awakening

- *Visualise your smiling face radiating with positive energy. Repeat silently three times,*
  "I am a peaceful soul. I am a powerful soul. I am a lovable soul."

- *When ready, I will count from one to three, and you will slowly open your eyes feeling refreshed, alert, and healthier than before.*

* *One... two... coming back slowly... three... eyes open, wide awake, feeling wonderful. Better than before. Do not open your eyes abruptly. Gently look down at your lap. Then slowly look up.*

Integration and Reflection

* Remember: practice daily, morning and evening, to deepen your connection with this powerful meditation tool.

* You now possess a technique to use your mind intentionally - for healing, intuition, and vividly creating your future.

* Care for your body with loving thoughts, good nutrition, and mindful movement.

* When challenges arise, anchor yourself in this meditative strength; guide your mind toward health and wellbeing confidently.

Creating Visualisation Zone & Spiritual Guides

(For detailed instructions, see Chapter 11)

Let's begin...

As you pass through the Resource Gateway into your Resource Center, you will connect with the positive energy patterns of all resources.

Use the 10-to-1 countdown to move through the Gateway and into your Resource Center... Lock three fingers. Take them close to your heart. I am going to go into my resource centre.

* *10, 9 - Physical resources like strength and vitality are present in me.*

* *8, 7 - Emotional resources like courage and compassion are present in me.*

* *6, 5, 4 - Intellectual resources like clarity and wisdom are present in me.*

* *3, 2, 1 - I possess intuitive and spiritual resources, such as intuition, healing, creativity, oneness, and purpose.*

Unlock your three fingers when you complete Resource Gateway.

Resource Center

You can furnish your resource centre in a way that helps encourage effective problem-solving. Suggestions for furnishing your resource centre are:

Lock three fingers. Take them close to your heart. I am going to create and furnish my Resource Center.

- *Comfortable chair*

- *Desk or Table*

- *Time-mechanism – past, present, and future*

- *Replicator machine – which replicates an event or situation.*

- *Laptop, printer – stores all your memories and projects.*

- *Medicine chest and toolbox.*

- *A unique area like a huge whiteboard or TV can focus on your visualisation zone for the transformation and manifestation of projects.*

- *Chairs for your spiritual guides and visitors.*

Sculpting Intuitive Consultants/Spiritual Guides

Creating Your Intuitive Male Consultant

- *Lock three fingers and bring them close to your heart. Say to yourself: "I am going to create my intuitive male consultant."*

- *While seated comfortably in your Resource Centre, choose a male role model or knowledgeable person you admire. Visualise him seated opposite you, either on your left or right side. Remember which side you choose.*

- *Affirm: "(Name of male) is my intuitive Male Consultant. He assists me with focus, concentration, desires, solutions, and advice in my best interest as well as for the greater good, for honest and positive outcomes only."*

- *When ready, count silently: 1, 2, 3. Slowly raise your arm and begin sculpting the male consultant with your eyes closed. Imagine and detail each part at your own comfortable pace: Head, hair (texture, length), face, nose, cheeks, Neck, shoulders, arms, wrists, hands, fingers, Chest, hips, thighs, knees, calves, ankles, heels, soles, feet, toes, nails...*

- *Once complete, review your sculpt and refine any features. When satisfied, count silently to three to finalise.*

- *Blow a breath of life into your consultant with a gentle "Pooh!" as he inhales the spark of life, becoming intelligent and alive.*

- *Greet him warmly and shake hands. Notice his response. You may ask his name and listen to his voice if needed.*

- *Remember, whenever you seek assistance, reassurance, intuitive, or creative ideas, you can communicate with your male consultant. Visualise him showing or telling you helpful insights. For male-related challenges, consult your male consultant.*

Creating Your Intuitive Female Consultant

- *Lock three fingers and bring them close to your heart. Say to yourself: "I am going to create my intuitive female consultant."*

- *Seated comfortably in your Resource Centre, select a female role model or wise person you value. Visualise her seated opposite you on either left or right side. Remember the side.*

- *Affirm: "(Name of female) is my intuitive Female Consultant. She assists me with focus, concentration, desires, solutions, and advice in my best interest and for honest positive results."*

- *Count silently: 1, 2, 3. Slowly raise your arm and start sculpting the female consultant with eyes closed. Visualise and shape her features at your pace: Head, hair (texture, length), face, nose, cheeks, Neck, shoulders, arms, wrists, hands, fingers, Chest, hips, thighs, knees, calves, ankles, heels, soles, feet, toes, nails...*

- *When finished, refine details as needed. Finalise on a silent count of three.*

- *Blow a breath of life into your consultant with a gentle "Pooh!" as she inhales the spark of life, intelligent and alive.*

- *Greet her warmly, offer a gesture like a hug, and observe her response. Ask her name and listen to her voice if necessary.*

- *Whenever you need support, reassurance, or creative ideas, communicate with your female consultant and imagine her offering guidance. For female-related issues, consult your female consultant.*

- *Finally, unlock your three fingers.*

Forgiveness

- *Silently forgive all who have hurt you, knowingly or unknowingly, and release them gently from your life.*

- *Invite forgiveness from all whom you may have hurt, knowingly or unknowingly.*

- *Forgiveness is much more than letting go; it is an act of love for the soul. It does not erase the past but allows us to view it with compassion and mercy. Forgiveness liberates your soul and dissolves fear.*

- *It is not just pardoning others but nurturing your own emotional wellbeing, a beautiful and permanent transformation, an acceptance of your inner power and unconditional love.*

- *Release your ego. Release your past. Seek forgiveness with complete faith and belief.*

Gratitude

- *Offer gratitude now: Thank you, Universe, God, Guru, Guides, Family, and Self for blessing me with a good heart, clear mind, strong hands, agile body, and steady legs. Thank you for nourishing food, clean air to breathe, and bountiful nature that supports my growth.*

- *Raise your right hand to your chest, palm facing outward.*

- *Visualise golden light flowing from your palm to Mother Earth. Bless the Earth with joy, healing, kindness, beauty, and peace. Bless all people with love and bliss.*

- *Say silently, "Thank you, thank you, thank you," for these priceless blessings.*

Closing Affirmations and Awakening

- *Visualise your smiling face radiating with positive energy. Repeat silently three times,*
  "I am a peaceful soul. I am a powerful soul. I am a lovable soul."

- *When ready, I will count from one to three, and you will slowly open your eyes feeling refreshed, alert, and healthier than before.*

- *One... two... coming back slowly... three... eyes open, wide awake, feeling wonderful. Better than before. Do not open your eyes abruptly. Gently look down at your lap. Then slowly look up.*

Closing Call-to-Action: Ignite Your Inner Power

Make meditation your daily ritual, even if it's just for a few minutes. Each session builds momentum, unlocking deeper layers of your mind's potential. Create a peaceful space, anchor yourself with your three fingers, and harness your imagination to sharpen focus and clarity.

Remember, transformation is a journey, be patient and compassionate with yourself. Celebrate small victories and stay committed. With consistent practice, you'll tap into your inner wisdom and strength like never before.

Your mind is your most powerful tool - fuel it with care and watch your life and leadership soar.

APPENDIX 4

Affirmations & Manifestations

~ Our consciousness creates our world, and with the proper training, you can develop the ability to shift your mind.

That single truth has transformed countless lives. It means that when you can vividly visualise yourself achieving a goal, you set unseen forces into motion. Every achievement begins as a vision in the mind before it appears in the world. You may need to learn new skills, gather resources, or overcome self-doubt, but the raw potential to turn your vision into reality already lies within you.

Affirmations and mindful visualisation are your mental blueprint for success. They nurture this potential by reprogramming your subconscious mind - aligning thoughts, emotions, and beliefs with your chosen outcomes. This appendix introduces *The Art of Affirmation Writing* along with guided meditations designed to help you activate your creative consciousness and manifest with clarity.

Think of affirmations as daily self-conversations that bridge your inner world and outer reality. Ask those who consistently lead with calm focus - athletes, entrepreneurs, creators, healers and most will admit they practise daily affirmations and mental imagery. These rituals help them stay centred and confident, even in demanding environments.

So, before you proceed, take a quiet breath.
Let your mind settle.
Because the power you seek isn't "out there" - it's already within you, waiting for your command.

The Art of Affirmation Writing

Why Affirmations?

Through years of coaching leaders, professionals, and homemakers alike, one discovery stands out: those who consciously engage in positive self-talk possess greater emotional resilience, sharper focus, and sustained motivation. Daily affirmations are not empty words; they are deliberate mental conditioning.

Used wisely, they help reframe your inner dialogue, dissolve limiting beliefs, and create momentum toward authentic success, the kind built on awareness and faith, not fear.

In this appendix, we'll explore:

- What affirmations are and how they work.

- How to write powerful affirmations that speak to your subconscious.

- The best times to practise them for maximum impact.

- Simple guided meditations to pair with your affirmations for deep manifestation.

What Are Affirmations?

An affirmation is a conscious statement you repeat to reinforce the reality you *wish to experience as true*. Each repetition replaces doubt with conviction, confusion with direction. Thought by thought, word by word, affirmations help you think, feel, and act from a space of inner alignment.

Affirmations are always expressed in the **present tense**, in **positive language**, and with **emotional conviction**.

For example: "I am so happy and grateful to see my book on the bestseller list."

What might sound simple is, in fact, profoundly transformative. When practised regularly, affirmations become the subconscious script of your life - one that magnetises opportunities, strengthens self-belief, and opens doors that once appeared invisible.

How to Write Affirmations?

Follow these eight essential guidelines to craft positive affirmations that will support your success and help you live your best life every day:

- **Begin with "I am."** These two simple words carry immense power, grounding your : affirmation in your present identity.

- **Use the present tense.** Speak as if you are already living your goal. This alignment activates your subconscious, motivating persistent action to bring your vision into reality.

- **Phrase affirmations positively.** Focus on what you want, not what you don't want. (For example, do not say, "I don't want to be stressed." Your mind hears "stressed." Instead, say, "I am calm and peaceful.")

- **Keep it simple.** Easy-to-memorise affirmations are easier to repeat and visualize, strengthening your subconscious programming.

- **Be specific.** Instead of a vague goal like "I am happy with my weight," say, "I am happy and grateful to have lost 25 pounds and fit into my favourite jeans." Clear visions inspire clearer actions.

- **Include an "-ing" action word.** Express your affirmation as an ongoing experience, e.g., "I am walking confidently across the stage to receive my degree."

- **Add emotional or feeling words.** Words like "happy," "grateful," and "joyful" heighten positive energy and help attract what you desire.

- **Make affirmations about yourself – not others.** You cannot control others' actions; only your own. Affirmations like "I am so happy now that my colleague is supportive" won't work. Instead, focus on your beliefs and behaviours.

Using these guidelines, your affirmations will become powerful tools to shape your thinking, emotions, and ultimately your life's outcomes.

Activity: Write 3 Powerful Affirmations for Yourself

To harness the true power of affirmations, try this practical exercise:

- Begin by identifying three meaningful goals you want to achieve in the next 12 months. What accomplishments would bring you true fulfilment or growth?

- For each goal, create a present-tense, positive affirmation that captures the feeling of already achieving it. Write these affirmations in your journal as follows:

  - **Goal 1:** "I am so happy and grateful now that I am [describe yourself experiencing or celebrating this accomplishment]."

  - **Goal 2:** "I am so happy and grateful now that I am [vividly imagine and record the achievement of your second goal]."

  - **Goal 3:** "I am so happy and grateful now that I am [bring your third, most important aspiration to life in words]."

- Place your affirmation journal beside your bed. Make it a daily ritual to read and reflect on your affirmations every morning when you wake and every night before sleep. In this way, your goals become the bookends of your day – creating focus, energy, and intention.

Let's get started: pause now, take a few moments to write your three affirmations, and set the course for a transformative year ahead.

Affirmations For Various Situations

Are you ready to witness the power of manifesting your dreams in real-time? In this chapter, we'll dive deep into the transformative power of Creative Visualisation, leveraging the incredible capabilities of our Subconscious Mind and the Power of Attraction to manifest success and abundance beyond our wildest dreams.

Whether new to visualisation or looking to enhance your practice, this resource offers invaluable insights and practical tips to help you manifest your deepest desires in a sub-conscious state (Alpha level).

Affirmations to Heal Yourself Instantly

Too often, we're told that "time heals all wounds." But in truth, time is external - your healing is an inside job. You hold the power to choose when, and how, to heal your emotional hurts.

Let's take a quiet moment together to teach your mind this gentle truth: you can release pain and discomfort without waiting for years to pass. With the right tools and self-awareness, every wound becomes an opportunity to cultivate resilience.

Begin by recalling a moment from your past - perhaps loss, disappointment, or grief. Bring it gently to mind, knowing you are safe now.

Settle comfortably in your chair and softly close your eyes. If you wear spectacles, feel free to remove them. Follow along at your own pace; if you lose track, simply return to the present step, holding a warm, open attitude throughout.

Take a slow, deep breath. Inhale… Exhale. Do this three times, allowing your body to relax.

Now, repeat these affirmations inwardly, as you breathe:

- *I am a powerfully resilient being.*

- *My mind is my ally. I choose to keep it peaceful and stable in every situation.*

- *Today, I look within - if there is any pain or grief still echoing from the past, I am ready to acknowledge it with compassion.*

- *I recognise that hurtful people and tough situations have crossed my path, but I do not wait for "time" to heal my heart. Healing is my choice - and I choose now, and with understanding.*

- *No one can truly hurt me. Everyone acts from their own perspective.*

- *The past is over. I accept it was part of my journey.*

- *I forgive myself for any pain I have made my own… it's over… it's gone.*

- *I am the master of my emotions. I choose what and who lives rent-free in my mind.*

- *From today, I write a new chapter of peace and happiness. I am free from past hurt.*

- *I create new karmic accounts of inner strength and positivity.*

Allow these words to settle. Now, as you finish, count up from one to five. With each number, feel lighter, clearer, and ready for a fresh beginning.

One... two... three... four... five.
Eyes open, feeling awake, refreshed, and filled with health and renewed well-being.

Remember: With intention and affirmation, healing is always within reach.

Forgiveness

- *Silently forgive all who have hurt you, knowingly or unknowingly, and release them gently from your life.*

- *Invite forgiveness from all whom you may have hurt, knowingly or unknowingly.*

- *Forgiveness is much more than letting go; it is an act of love for the soul. It does not erase the past but allows us to view it with compassion and mercy. Forgiveness liberates your soul and dissolves fear.*

- *It is not just pardoning others but nurturing your own emotional wellbeing, a beautiful and permanent transformation, an acceptance of your inner power and unconditional love.*

- *Release your ego. Release your past. Seek forgiveness with complete faith and belief.*

Gratitude

- *Offer gratitude now: Thank you, Universe, God, Guru, Guides, Family, and Self for blessing me with a good heart, clear mind, strong hands, agile body, and steady legs. Thank you for nourishing food, clean air to breathe, and bountiful nature that supports my growth.*

- *Raise your right hand to your chest, palm facing outward.*

- *Visualise golden light flowing from your palm to Mother Earth. Bless the Earth with joy, healing, kindness, beauty, and peace. Bless all people with love and bliss.*

- *Say silently, "Thank you, thank you, thank you," for these priceless blessings.*

Closing Affirmations and Awakening

- *Visualise your smiling face radiating with positive energy. Repeat silently three times, "I am a peaceful soul. I am a powerful soul. I am a lovable soul."*

- *When ready, I will count from one to three, and you will slowly open your eyes feeling refreshed, alert, and healthier than before.*

- *One… two… coming back slowly… three… eyes open, wide awake, feeling wonderful. Better than before. Do not open your eyes abruptly. Gently look down at your lap. Then slowly look up.*

Affirmations for Creating Abundance – Thought, Attitude, and Belief

(For detailed instructions, see Chapter 8)

In this affirmation practice, you'll train your mind to picture and experience your deepest desires – money, health, love, and meaningful relationships, on your inner mental screen. If visual imagery feels difficult, use sounds and sensations; the point is to immerse yourself in the feeling of already living your ideal life.

- *Start by sitting comfortably and gently close your eyes. Take a deep belly breath, letting go of any tension or pressure. Allow your breath to become slow and rhythmic, relaxing your mind and body with each exhale.*

- *Imagine yourself in a tranquil, positive state. See yourself thriving, happy, and successful living the life you want. If any thoughts of lack or limitation arise, notice them honestly and then let them go. Picture yourself breaking through those old beliefs, watching new doors of opportunity swing open. With every breath, remind yourself: you are free to choose your attitude and transform your reality.*

- *Take a moment to see your life unfolding as you want it - abundant, joyful, and deeply satisfying. See yourself already embodying the success, happiness, and relationships you desire. Seal that vision; let your future and present become one in your mind.*

- *Experience the freedom to live a life filled with joy, love, abundance, and vibrant health. Imagine your relationships, your work, and your wellbeing getting stronger day by day, because you choose to believe in your own potential.*

- *Whenever you want to reinforce this state, press three fingers together on either hand. Use this anchor to return to your empowered mindset throughout the day.*

- *Repeat these affirmations silently:*
  - *I am creating a life of abundance, happiness, and love.*
  - *I choose my attitude and shift into positivity whenever I wish.*
  - *Each day, I grow healthier, wealthier, and more fulfilled.*
  - *My relationships blossom with joy and understanding.*
  - *I am free to thrive, to love, and to succeed.*

- *Seal this feeling within. When you're ready, slowly open your eyes. Carry the energy of your empowered state into each moment, as if what you desire has already come true.*

Practicing this daily affirms that your life is unfolding exactly as you intend - programming your mind for success, happiness, and abundance.

Affirmations for Inner Reflection

As you relax, reflect on the past 24-48 hours: the events, thoughts, and interactions you've had - positive or negative, with family, friends, and others. Notice any emotional obstacles: fear, anger, doubt, grief, or old frustrations.

- *Settle into a comfortable chair and gently close your eyes. Remove your spectacles if you wear them and simply listen along; it's fine if you miss a step - just continue at your pace, holding a cheerful, open spirit.*

- *Begin with three deep, steady breaths. Inhale… exhale… let tension dissolve with each breath. If you notice anger, frustration, or any agitation, focus on slow breathing and exhale all the unwanted energy.*

- *Picture a whiteboard about six feet in front of your closed eyes. Place those negative emotions and experiences onto this mental screen. Imagine picking up a duster and gently wiping the board clean. Visualise all negative energy dissolving and being released into space.*

- *Repeat this cleansing action three to five times, until the whiteboard feels refreshed and clear. Now, mentally cut the cord connecting you to those old emotions - visualise snipping away attachment to negativity.*

- *Welcome loving-kindness into your mind, words, intentions, and actions. Release guilt and self-criticism. Embrace non-judgment, compassion, and positive intentions. Fill your body and mind with total relaxation and lightness.*

- *Imagine a shower of radiant light flowing from above, bathing every cell in energy and wellbeing. Absorb that sensation, as you trust your inner connection to the universe, your guides, and yourself.*

- *Know that your best intentions matter—for yourself, others, and the world. Rest in stillness, aware of brilliant light and openness.*

- *When you're ready, slowly count up: one, two, three. Open your eyes, feeling healthy, peaceful, and ready to move forward with the intention of serving humanity in all you do.*

Affirmations for Maitri Bhav – Loving Kindness

In Buddhism, loving-kindness (Maitri) is the foundation of the Four Immeasurable - four core virtues that nourish both your own well-being and harmonious relationships with others:

- Loving-Kindness (Maitri)

- Compassion

- Sympathetic Joy

- Equanimity

As teachers like Longchenpa and Acharya Goenka remind us, Maitri begins not with others, but with yourself. "To have compassion for others, we must first have compassion for ourselves." The journey of befriending yourself sets the stage for every other form of kindness.

Maitri for Oneself

- *Silently or aloud, repeat these affirmations as you settle into a comfortable, relaxed state: "I am happy, healthy, safe, and living with ease."*

- *If you notice a negative thought spiral, return to: "I am happy."*

- *If facing physical challenges: "I am healthy and strong."*

- *In difficult or unsafe relationships: "I am safe."*

- *During moments of stress or anxiety: "I am living with ease."*

Maitri for Others

- *Now, extend Maitri to those close to you – your parents, spouse, children, siblings, or anyone in your immediate circle. Affirm: "They (say their names) are happy, healthy, safe, and living with ease."*

- *Next, direct Maitri towards a neutral person or someone with whom you share friction: "He/She (name) is happy, healthy, safe, and living with ease."*

- *Expand your loving-kindness outward – to your community, city, nation, and the entire universe – embracing all living and non-living beings: "They are happy, healthy, safe, and living with ease."*

- *Express gratitude for this practice, and if you wish, silently seek forgiveness for any harm, real or imagined. Gently open your eyes when finished.*

Remember: Repetition is transformative. Notice when your self-talk turns less than friendly and use these affirmations – aloud or silently, as a gentle reset throughout your day. Your Maitri Bhav, cultivated within, naturally radiates to all around you.

Benefits of Daily Affirmations

Research shows that daily repetition of positive affirmations can break negative thinking patterns and boost self-esteem. With a stronger sense of self-worth, you'll feel more confident taking risks and can achieve better results in all areas of life.

Here are some key benefits you'll gain from a regular affirmation practice:

- **Combats Negative Self-Talk:** By affirming positive beliefs, you become more aware of your internal dialogue and can quickly catch negative thoughts. Affirmations help replace self-doubt with empowering messages, keeping you focused on what truly matters.

- **Reduces Stress:** Negative thinking triggers the body's fight-or-flight response, making it hard to stay calm and think clearly. Positive affirmations shift this response by helping you feel proud of who you are, reducing stress and fostering focus.

- **Eases Anxiety:** Studies show that replacing negative thoughts with positive ones and visualizing desired outcomes helps people with anxiety remain calm and centered during stressful situations.

- **Lifts Depression:** Our brains naturally highlight threats and negatives more than positives, a survival mechanism. Affirmations help counter this negativity bias, shifting your focus toward hope and possibility.

- **Enhances Overall Wellbeing:** Lower stress and anxiety levels encourage better sleep, healthier eating, and more motivation to maintain an active, balanced lifestyle.

Making a habit of positive self-affirmation rewires your mind to view yourself and your world more optimistically. This shift boosts your self-esteem, nurtures self-respect, and supports consistent self-care - fostering lasting transformation and success.

Examples of Daily Affirmations

To inspire your own affirmation practice for success, here are some vivid examples:

- *"I am joyfully driving my new red Audi convertible down the Goa Highway or Pacific Coast Highway."*
  If you prefer eco-friendly options, swap the car for a new Tesla, Ford Mustang Mach-E, or Hyundai Kona electric.

- *"I am so happy and grateful to be thriving in my chosen career, earning Rs One crore or $150,000 a year."*

- *"I am so happy and grateful to be celebrating my ideal weight of 65 kg or 140 pounds."*

- *"I am enjoying my beautiful beachfront villa on Bali Island or somewhere even more magical."*

This last affirmation is particularly special to me. I began writing it for myself in 1999, and by 2001, it had become my reality! My shipping company gave me an assignment to take over a ship based in Bali.

These examples illustrate how detailed, sensory-rich affirmations help you vividly imagine your desired life, an essential step toward manifesting it.

It's time to discover the secret to deliberately creating and receiving more of what you want in life!

You must be congruent about how you think to keep it positive. Keep your attitude great. Let your beliefs open doors of opportunity. Let your behaviour support you along the way. Because you know, and I know, you can have it all or better… and better.

Recommendations For Further Study

For those eager to deepen their journey in mindset, meditation, and personal growth, here are some inspiring resources – that have enriched the MindRetreat community.

Biographies and Success Stories: The seeds of success are sown in the mind. Reading about the journeys of remarkable individuals can help those seeds sprout and flourish in your own life. Recommended Books:

- *Vipassana Meditation* by S.N. Goenka & William Hart
- *Vedanta Treatise – The Eternities* by Swami A. Parthasarathy
- *Bhagavad Gita* by Swami A. Parthasarathy
- *How Do You Know What You Know* by Janki Santoke
- *The Power of One Thought* by BK Shivani
- *Play of Conscious Mind* by Swami Muktananda
- *Autobiography of a Yogi* by Paramhansa Yogananda
- *Yoga Nidra* by Swami Satyananda Saraswati
- *Preksha Meditation* by Acharya Mahapragya
- *Unlimited Power* by Anthony Robbins
- *Atomic Habits* by James Clear
- *The Secret* by Rhonda Byrne
- *The Magic of Thinking Big* by David J. Schwartz
- *The Power of Your Subconscious Mind* by Joseph Murphy
- *Creative Visualisation* by Shakti Gawain
- *Think and grow Rich* by Napolean Hill
- *The Art of War* by Sun Tzu

Let these books and stories inspire new perspectives, habits, and possibilities as you continue your journey of self-discovery and transformation.

Acknowledgments

I want to thank my wife, Shail, and my children, Pracchi, Amrish, Nakuul, and Jankee, for their support and suggestions. They created an environment where I could let my creative juices flow at any hour of the day or night and have my ideas received by sympathetic ears.

The trainers, coaches, and colleagues: Dr Swati Lodha, Dr Saumya Badgaiyan, Asif Ebrahim, Dr Shanker Vishwanath, and Riddhi Doshi, whose personalities, methods, and friendships have affected me most in writing this book and can never be forgotten.

I am grateful to Dr Anjana Vinod for many of the reflections from her stories.

Special thanks to MindRetreat – participants worldwide, who daily support me in conducting online Mindful Meditation sessions – Dr Saroj Modi (Gurugram), Dilip Dhadda (Hyderabad), Pooran Chugani (Los Angeles), Sheetal Jogia (London), Pravesh Sawon (Mauritius), Shama Gandhi (Los Angles), Kalindi Multani (Chicago), Loretta DeSa (N Carolina), Prakash Bhatia (New Jersey), Jayashree Modha (Nairobi), Usha Sukumaran (Melbourne, Aus), Unnati Priya (Varanasi), Humera Nizam Shah (Mumbai), Uma Shivprasad (Mysore), Sangita Gandhi (Mysore), Simranjit Kaur (Malaysia), Prerana Sharma (Udaipur) and many more.

About the Author

~ #1 Success Coach | Author | Mindset Alchemist |
Storyteller | Navy Veteran

What does it take to weather a midnight storm at sea? Then guide others through their inner tempests. Capt Pratap Mehta knows firsthand.

A decorated Indian Navy veteran of the 1971 Indo-Pak War. He led teams through chaos with steady resolve. Drawing from Vedic and Buddhist wisdom. Today he channels that clarity into transformation. Military precision meets practical coaching.

Known for charismatic communication. Relatable approach. He distils complex psychology into everyday strategies.

As an author, Capt Mehta brought Rajasthan's vibrant past untold stories to life in the acclaimed:

- *Rajputana Chronicles: Guns and Glories* (2016)

- *Parakram aur Parampara* (Hindi, 2023)

Graduate in Nautical Science and Strategic Studies. Master's in Defence Studies from Defence Services Staff College. HR Management from NMIMS, Mumbai. Keynote speaker from London to Mauritius. Visiting faculty. Lifelong history student.

Curious how a Navy Commander became a celebrated mindset coach? Join MindRetreat workshops, online sessions, talks. He equips people to thrive through life's storms.

Connect:

captainpsm@gmail.com

LinkedIn – **https://www.linkedin.com/in/pratapmehta/**